Taking Running Records

A teacher shares her experience on how to take running records and use what they tell you to assess and improve every child's reading

SCHOLASTIC
PROFESSIONAL BOOKS

NEW YORK • TORONTO • LONDON • AUCKLAND • SYDNEY
MEXICO CITY • NEW DELHI • HONG KONG

DEDICATION

This book is dedicated to all the special people who help readers grow.

ACKNOWLEDGMENTS

I have always felt that none of our accomplishments is a solo event. There are people who have directly and indirectly influenced us on our way toward a goal. They provide the "wind beneath the wings."

I thank family, friends, and colleagues for the day-to-day sunshine and support in my life. I haven't met all the people with whom I've worked at Scholastic, but I can tell from our phone conversations, e-mails, and letters that they are very efficient and caring. I'd like to thank Joanna Davis-Swing and Jeanette Moss for all their feedback. I especially wish to thank Terry Cooper for the opportunity to share my experiences through this text and Wendy Murray for insights and suggestions offered so graciously. I've also loved learning "publisher talk" from Scholastic editors. I share it with my students.

Most of all, I wish to acknowledge the students I've had the privilege of working with. I've learned so much from them. I could not have written this book without them.

Cover photograph by Nina Roberts
Interior design by Solutions by Design, Inc.

ISBN 0-439-07752-4

Table of Contents

CHAPTER 5

Putting It All Together

CHAPTER 6

Looking Closer

CHAPTER 7

Using Running Records to Inform Your Teaching

Bibliography

Introduction

In my experience as a teacher, I've not found a single assessment that gives as much information on a child's literacy development as a running record (RR). Introduced by Marie M. Clay, it is the most efficient, quick way of gathering reliable data that is customized to the learner. Results are immediately available.

RRs reveal skills and strategies the child uses to decode, comprehend, and interpret different kinds and levels of text read orally or silently. In the world outside of school, we read to understand and retell personal interpretations of what we read, to inform others, or to share a selection we particularly enjoyed. The process of taking a running record mirrors that experience—matching the way reading unfolds in everyday situations.

The process of taking a RR is also nonthreatening. You can easily establish a high degree of comfort for the child. Test anxiety seldom inhibits performance to deflate overall scores. In fact, the interaction involved in taking a running-record assessment is a bonding experience for the teacher and child. The two collaborate on analyzing the child's performance. The child is encouraged to take control—construct personal meanings and use errors to apply correcting skills. The teacher and child talk about the child's reading performance and what it reveals—strengths and needs.

Like learning any skill, learning how to take accurate and useful records may at first appear daunting, but running records become very doable when you allow yourself to progress step by step at your own pace. Take advantage of support systems. Invite the children's help. Assisting you as you take the record gives them insights about the process while bolstering their confidence as they progress. Working with colleagues to make the use of running records a school-wide effort creates another source of support.

Be as patient with yourself as you are with learners. Be as persistent as you want learners to be when facing challenging tasks. I've always found that placing myself in a learning situation, especially one that is difficult (i.e., mastering the computer) reinforces my level of empathy for students. Students have always been sympathetic supporters while I worked at mastering new teaching skills. They have no trouble identifying with my challenge.

I hope that by sharing my own experiences with learning and using running records I will help to guide you as you take the plunge.

Above all, enjoy helping readers grow!

Timetable for Learning, Taking, and Using Running Records

Start the second week of school, after building a comfortable tone.

While you work one-to-one with students, other students are:

❈ working at learning centers.

❈ working independently (i.e., response activities related to content area or literature studies).

❈ silently reading during D.E.A.R. (Drop Everything And Read) time.

❈ working on personal writing pieces.

WEEK IN SCHOOL YEAR	ACTIVITY
Weeks 1–2	Help students learn to work independently at centers. Establish classroom routines so you will have uninterrupted time to take running records
Week 3	Listen to a child read and retell the text selection read. Take anecdotal notes on the child's performance. Work with one child at a time—one per day. (5 completed)
Week 4	Listen to a child read and retell the text selection read. Take anecdotal notes on the child's performance. Work with one child at a time—one per day. (5 completed)
Week 5	Listen to a child read and retell the text selection read. Take anecdotal notes on the child's performance. Work with one child at a time—one per day. (5 completed)
Week 6	Listen to a child read and retell the text selection read. Take anecdotal notes on the child's performance. Work with one child at a time—two per day. (10 completed)
Week 7	Practice using the marking system during the oral reading, and take anecdotal notes on the retelling. Then you can check your work by listening to the tape. Work with one child at a time—one per day. (5 completed)
Week 8	Listen to a child read and retell the text selection read. Tape the session. Take a RR on the oral reading and anecdotal notes on a general retelling. Work with one child at a time—two per day. (10 completed)
Week 9	Listen to a child read and retell the text selection read. Tape the session. Take a RR on the oral reading and anecdotal notes on a general retelling. Work with one child at a time—two per day. (10 completed)

Week 10	You have rich information on children's literacy development for quarterly reports to parents. Introduce, model, and practice the retelling process. Review graphic organizers and model their use in guiding a retelling.
Week 11	Introduce the retelling checklists. Model their use for evaluating a retelling. Have students practice retelling and evaluating the teacher's retelling and each other's retelling.
Week 12	Do a complete RR—record the oral reading and complete a checklist for the retelling. Tape the session. Work with one child at a time—one per day. (5 completed)
Week 13	Do a complete RR—record the oral reading and complete a checklist for the retelling. Tape the session. Work with one child at a time—one per day. (5 completed)
Week 14	Do a complete RR—record the oral reading and complete a checklist for the retelling. Tape the session. Work with one child at a time—one per day. (5 completed)
Week 15	Do a complete RR—record the oral reading and complete a checklist for the retelling. Tape the session. Work with one child at a time—two per day. (10 completed)

Do a complete running record—week 12-15 cycle—again at the end of the school year for all children and more frequently for struggling readers.

Much like a court stenographer's notes, a running record provides a word-for-word accounting of what was said.

Running Record Recording Form

Reader __Jamie__   Gr. _1_   Date _____   Recorder _____

Text Read__Shadows Are About__   Familiar _✓_ Unfamiliar ____ Genre **concept book**

Accuracy: _90_%   SC: 7/3   E freq: 1/10 every 10th word   Reading rate: ___ fast _✓_ av. ___ slow   Text level: **K-1**

Comprehension: ____ full _✓_ satisfactory ____ fragmented or % ____ on questions asked

Comments __Used picture clues effectively. Several miscues maintained meaning—i.e. stand for stretch. Breaks up compound words with pause between—but not smooth. Uses strategy of covering up ½ of compound word, decoding each part, then blending. Not 'stopping in tracks' with longer words now.__

Reading level for this text: ____ independent _✓_ instructional ____ frustrational

Pg.		# E	# SC	\multicolumn{3}{Error match}
				M	S	L-S
1	✓✓ ✓✓ ✓✓					
3	In...side✓ out...side✓ ✓✓ around / Inside outside about	1				
5	✓✓✓✓✓ swing/away ✓✓	1				
7	✓ drop/droop ✓✓✓✓ ✓✓	1				
9	✓ stand/stretch ✓✓✓ ch...th...run/chase ✓✓	2				
10	✓✓ ✓✓ ✓✓ ✓					
12	✓ ✓ ✓ sk...sk..ip✓ / skip					
13	some...times✓ / sometimes ✓ (turn) ✓✓ R	1				
14	✓ #14/flap ✓✓	1				
15	✓ swing/swoop ✓✓	1				
16	✓✓✓ ✓					
17	✓✓✓					
18	✓✓ ✓✓					
	✓ m..m...A..I/march be-side✓ / beside ✓✓	1				

62   *Taking Running Records* Scholastic Professional Books

CHAPTER 1

Assessing Reading Growth With Running Records

"Yet a funny thing happens on the way to those final assessments: day-to-day learning takes place. I am certain that, in education, evaluation needs to pay more attention to the systematic observation of learners who are on their way to those final assessments."

(Clay, 1987, p. 1)

Step-by-step assessment of children's learning can be the stitch in time that makes the difference for young readers. As I watch my students day to day and throughout the year, they reveal their understanding in words and performances. By documenting facts that accumulate and strengths that emerge, I can integrate what I learn to create a complete picture of each child's level of competence as the year progresses. Reflecting on this knowledge, I can direct my teaching to give appropriate support in a timely way—to plan lessons to reteach, reinforce, or extend learning. I can adjust the sequence of instruction to take advantage of teachable moments that increase the children's motivation and the likelihood that they will be successful learners.

The methods and purpose of such ongoing, classroom-based assessment differ notably from the external, standardized tests schools traditionally depend on to confirm literacy growth. Those tests yield information for curriculum development. They identify strengths and weaknesses in a district's program when grade and school scores are compared to regional, state, and national norms. They also identify where a child stands in comparison to other students and generate reference points for a child's academic growth in core curricular areas over an extended period of time. However, when such norm-referenced scores are used to examine an individual learner's achievement, supporting or contradicting evidence based on day-to-day classroom assessment should be provided. But why wait until traditional standardized tests indicate that children have gotten lost in their literacy development when immediate assessments can reveal a need for intervention?

Teachers have always watched their students' development, but have not always trusted the reliability of their observations. This lack of confidence is gradually dissipating as systematic observation becomes a more acceptable method of assessment, particularly in early childhood education (Barr, Craig, Fisette, & Syverson, 1999; Clay, 1993; *"Primary Language Record,"* 1989). Teachers are now using a variety of formalized classroom observational practices to gather evidence of achievement as children go about the business of learning in the comfort of a classroom setting. Consistent guidelines and routines ensure detailed analysis of literacy growth across settings. Effective tools, systematically applied in the assessment process, are integral to the overall validity of information classroom teachers can gather. Running records (RR) are one such tool.

What Are Running Records?

In *An Observational Survey of Early Literacy Achievement* (1993), Marie Clay presents the running record, a method she developed for determining a child's reading competence at a given moment in time with a specific level and type of book. To create a running record, the teacher sits with the child and uses specific shorthand, or codes, to record detailed information while the child reads aloud. The resulting record provides the teacher with a playback of an entire oral reading episode, including the smallest details on the reader's attitude, demeanor, accuracy, and understanding. With the record in hand, the teacher can analyze behaviors, responses, competencies, initiatives taken, and understanding of the specific content and task. Because these codes are standardized, they are consistent across settings and among teachers.

The teacher uses the running record to calculate scores, analyze errors, and document strategies the child uses to successfully decode words and construct meaning. The notations, although in shorthand, are detailed enough to provide a multi-layered account of the child's performance in oral reading, comprehension of main idea and details, and ability to interpret and draw logical conclusions when reading different kinds of books (i.e., story, informational, poetry).

The Benefits of Using Running Records

They Are Authentic

Authenticity in assessment refers to the degree that the instrument used and the information gained from it measure the child's performance of a particular skill in *everyday* use. If the instrument, content, or format of an assessment task differs considerably from the way the child uses the skill in routine situations, the information is flawed and should not be used. An authentic assessment such as running records creates a unique and detailed picture as the interaction between teacher and learner unfolds. For the child, such interactive assessment is "just another practice of what I do all the time." The only difference is that the teacher is giving greater attention to the child and will be making notations during the performance. Conversations that arise focus on the content of the task, though the child may make comments about some other aspect of her reading that the teacher can make note of and follow up on later. This kind of collaboration is a cornerstone of authentic assessment—assessment that will enable children to gradually monitor their own learning.

They Create a Dialogue Between Teacher and Student

The first few times I take a running record with a child, I explain why we're doing it, what she needs to do, and what I'll be doing. For example:

> Today I'd like you to read aloud for me while the other [children] are working. While you read from this book on spiders, I'll be making marks for the words you say. I want to see how smoothly you read—if you read in phrases that sound like talking—and how you figure out words, how you use expression and how you pay attention to punctuation. When you get to this page, you can stop and tell me all about what you read, as if I were someone who had never heard it before. You'll be showing me what you can already do and what I should help you with next. When you're finished, I'll show you the marks and explain what they mean.

Explaining what's happening keeps the recording from being a mystery to the child and allays any fears she may have about being graded or judged; the child trusts that the teacher will explain the marks. After children have experienced the process and observed me working with others a few times, explanations become less necessary.

A powerful—and joyful—side effect of this assessment process is the opportunity for teacher-student bonding. The child is performing solo—soaking up positive attention from the teacher. The relationship becomes stronger, and the child is more willing to accept the teacher's suggestions for improvement in this climate. The dialogue that accompanies the interaction guides the child's thinking about what a reader does to construct meaning and strengthens her ability to assess her own performance.

They Celebrate Strengths

When the child completes the reading and has retold the story, the teacher shares and discusses the record with her. The discussion starts with compliments that illustrate exactly what the child did well: *Your reading was smooth and you grouped words together this time to make it sound more like talking. I liked the way you used expression in the scary part.*

They Provide the Child With Immediate, Detailed Feedback

After pointing out strengths, the teacher gives feedback that includes sensitively stated comments on specific areas of difficulty. Teacher and child discuss errors (miscues) made in the reading. The analysis includes scaffolded corrections pointing out how the error could have been avoided or self-corrected. For example:

Teacher: You skipped this word when you read. Here's where I marked it as a missed word. Do you know it?

Child: No.

T: How can you figure it out?

C: Sound it out?

T: You can look at the letters and think about the sounds for those letters. What else can you think about that will help you figure it out?

C: Use the Clunk list (see list on page 17).
Mmmmm...think about what's happening. Look at the picture.

T: Those are good places for clues that you can match with the sound clues. Reread this part and use your ideas to figure it out.

C: The dinosaur had a strong, mmm.../sh/...mmmmm...oh I know—sharp beak, because...look...it's pointed in the picture and he's cutting the branch with it!

T: Good for you! You thought about what other word would describe his beak and looked at the illustration for clues to match the starting /sh/ sound.

Sometimes I use this kind of teachable moment to conduct an on-the-spot mini-lesson. For example:

T: Keep in mind what the part you're reading is mostly about and use picture clues. This will make it easier to figure out words as you go. The word can't be any word in the world. It has to make sense and sound right—like the way we talk in a sentence. If your brain is expecting certain words because of what it's all about, your eyes will recognize the word faster when you see it—even just the first few letters of it.

Keep Interventions During a Running Record Session Brief

Generally it's best to let the reader finish his reading of a RR text on his own. But if he stops and is unable or unwilling to attack a word, you will have to help.

1 Prompt or guide the child to independently apply strategies that may help: *When you skipped the word* sharp, *the rest of the sentence didn't make sense. What can you do when you don't know a word?* With meaningful and positive coaching, a blend of compliments and comments, children grow in their ability to use the strategies they've learned to assess their own performance. This thinking about thinking, or metacognitive behavior, is a cornerstone of independence as a reader.

2 If the child needs more help, make your instructional point short and specific: *When you don't know a word, reread the sentence. And remember, meaning helps you figure out a word you don't know. Think about what it could be. Then use letter-sound clues to decide if your prediction is right or if you need to try another word. Think about what you're reading as you go along so that you understand how each part connects to the next.*

3 Conclude the interaction with a goal for reading practice: *The next time you read for me, we'll try this strategy to figure out a word you get stuck on.*

Using Running Records to Diagnose Needs and Plan Teaching

Running records provide some quantified results (i.e., scores for accuracy in word reading and comprehension of text), but they are basically qualitative in nature. Besides providing useful diagnostic information on the process the child uses to read at particular levels with particular text structures, RRs monitor which strategies a child tries during the reading act and what he does if a strategy isn't working.

Monitoring a child's strategy use—how he thinks through a text—during the reading act adds rich insights on his current level of literacy achievement. Instruction that applies this information, or diagnostic teaching (Walker, 1996, p.3), is focused on the child's needs and ensures growth toward independence. Running records can be used as a tool for diagnostic teaching that is responsive to those teachable moments when learners are ripe for specific instruction. In a diagnostic model, the teacher monitors the child's progress *within* the interaction, determining what has been learned and what has not. Further teaching adjusts accordingly.

Classroom teachers also use the results of running records to guide decisions related to:

Evaluating the Difficulty Level (Independent, Instructional or Frustrational) of a Particular Text for the Reader

Make the Text Fit the Reader

The following guidelines can help you in this process.

❊ **Independent-level** text can be read independently by the child. Texts at this level are appropriate for Sustained Silent-Reading (SSR) time.

❊ **Instructional-level** texts can be read by the child if the teacher or peers provide support. Texts at this level offer an appropriate challenge and should be used in guided reading.

❊ **Frustrational-level** texts are too difficult for the child at this time, even with help. Because children's listening levels are usually higher than their reading levels, texts at this level may be appropriate for teacher read-alouds. Read-alouds of high-interest texts—those that would be frustrating for a child to read himself—motivate, build knowledge, and offer a preview of literature that awaits the growing reader.

Grouping Children for Instruction

Grouping should be flexible—based on interest and needs that change across content and skill areas. Children should have opportunities to interact with all learners in their classroom community.

Monitoring Growth in Reading Skills and Strategies

Running records yield evidence of progress, interests, attitudes, and developing metacognitive strengths. Metacognition involves the learner's growing ability to reflect on his ideas, his awareness of how to accomplish a task, and his ability to monitor progress toward the completion of the task.

Observing Children's Particular Strengths and Difficulties

As the child applies problem-solving strategies in decoding the book's/text's message and constructing meaning, the teacher gains insights into his thinking. Precisely when, where, and how accurate word reading and efficient meaning processing break down becomes strikingly evident. The child demonstrates current literacy knowledge and level of performance on specific skills and strategies. For example, the teacher gains insights into how the child *orchestrates* semantic cues (meaning), syntactic cues (grammatical: What kind of word would go here to make it sound right—the way we talk?), and visual cues(letter/sound associations). Being able to coordinate the cues automatically in word recognition is key to fluency in reading.

The information gained from running records allows me to plan lessons

Orchestrating a Medley of Cues

Suppose a child needs to figure out what word comes after: Bears live in the (_____).

❊ Using semantic cues, he can begin to figure out what the word might be. Knowing that the next word can't be "any word in the world" makes the task of figuring it out less daunting. I encourage children: *Get your brain thinking of words that would make sense with other words in the sentence.*

❊ Using syntactic cues, he is aware that the kind of word that would make sense would have to be a place or thing (noun). Or that it might be a word that describes that place or thing (adjective). It couldn't be an action word (verb), because that doesn't sound right.

❊ Using semantic and syntactic cues together as context clues, the child narrows the possibilities of what the word could logically be and predicts that the next word might be *cage, cave, zoo, woods,* or *forest.*

❊ Using visual cues he can test those words. I remind the children: *Use your eyes to see if the letters you'd need for one of those words are on the page in that place. If your brain is thinking of a word, your eyes will recognize it faster. When possible words are in your mind, it's easier to recognize which one [is being used].*

❊ The child may think "woods," but see c-a-v-e. Since he is unable to confirm his prediction based on the letters he sees, visual, graphophonemic information (phonics—letter/sound knowledge) causes him to change the predicted word rather than confirm it in this instance.

that meet children's needs. I have documented detailed evidence of the child's performance in an act of reading, which I can share in a conference with his parents. After making parents aware of their child's strengths and weaknesses, we can talk about specific literacy goals and how they can support the child at home. Parents always find this information more useful than percentiles and stanine scores. To help parents get a sense of how running records work, I send them a letter similar to the one at the end of this chapter in advance of a parent-teacher conference.

Integrating Running Records for a Total Literacy Assessment

There are three important steps in using RRs as a tool for assessing children's literacy growth:

❉ taking the running record

❉ assessing the child's understanding through his retelling of the text he's read (see Chapter 4 for more about retelling)

❉ using the RR to pinpoint the child's word reading errors through detailed miscue analysis (see Chapter 6)

Running records, accompanied by story retellings and miscue analysis, create a record of literacy growth over time. The oral reading yields an accuracy score for decoding, while the retelling reveals the depth of comprehension. When retelling, the child is encouraged to explain what the text was mostly about, relate significant details, and share personal reactions or interpretations. A retelling can also be done with books that the child has read silently. To evaluate listening comprehension, a child may be asked to retell a passage that was read aloud by the teacher or peer. A follow-up miscue analysis provides a closer, line-by-line look at the kinds of decoding errors readers make.

This book will describe how you can record a child's oral reading in a way that allows a replay of the entire event for further detailed analysis. It will help you make decisions that are guided by children's performances. You will be able to integrate findings from day-to-day observations as you plan, implement, and modify meaningful classroom activities and instructional interactions with children.

Chapters 2–5 introduce running records in steps, encouraging practice with each until you're comfortable. You can move at your own pace. Chapter 6 explains how to analyze the data you gather. Chapter 7 describes how to use the information to plan the next instructional step and provides my responses to specific running-record scenarios.

It takes practice to become comfortable with taking RRs, but teachers quickly realize the benefits. The process generates information on several aspects of a reader's performance in a brief amount of time. I found that I could easily complete a RR for each student at the beginning and end of an academic year or for a given reporting period if more frequent records were needed. Once you get the procedures down, running records become a routine event in your classroom.

Word Recognition Strategy

Several years ago at a conference, a teacher-presenter shared this word recognition strategy with the audience. I made some modifications and used it successfully with students. It's a great way to build students' independence with word recognition and their ability to cross-check clues.

Provide abundant demonstrations of this strategy before you invite children to use it independently. Post this list in the classroom as a reference.

Before beginning running records, make parents aware of the strategies you're modeling and expectations you have for readers.

❉ A CLUNK is a word that stops you in your tracks . . .

❉ What To Do When You Meet a **CLUNK**:

1 Say mmm … and keep going to the end of the sentence with the **CLUNK** while thinking about the meaning. Reread the sentence with the **CLUNK** while thinking about the meaning clues you now have.

2 "Crash into" the **CLUNK**. Make your mouth say the sound for the letters at the beginning of the **CLUNK** while you look across the rest of the word.

3 If you still haven't figured it out, put in a word that would make sense and read on.

4 Ask someone about the **CLUNK** word when you've finished reading, and learn the new word.

Dear Parents:

I will be taking a running record of your child's oral reading and assessing his or her retelling of the reading during the weeks before quarterly reports. I'll share the results with you during our conference.

Running records are a tool I use to determine your child's reading competence with specific levels (degree of difficulty) and types of books. To take a record, I use a code to record detailed information while your child reads aloud from the book.

Here are examples of the coding:

❧ Words read correctly are coded with a check	✔✔✔✔✔
❧ Words misread (miscues or errors) are recorded by writing in the word the reader said with the word in the book below it.	reader: house text home
❧ When your child self-corrects a mistake, the error is crossed out and the letters sc are written in.	sc reader: ~~house~~ text home
❧ When your child inserts a word, it's written above a caret, and when a word is omitted, it's written in with a circle drawn around it.	the (new) ^

The record helps me see how well your child uses strategies to read words accurately and smoothly. When the oral reading is finished, I'll ask your child to tell me all about what was read as though I was someone who hadn't heard it before. This retelling reflects how well your child understands what she or he reads. I've been emphasizing the importance of thinking about what we're reading. The children understand that saying the words correctly is not enough.

When we meet for your child's progress conference, I'll share a complete running record with you—the most recent one. I'll also have you watch a video clip of the interaction while you follow along with the running-record markings. I'm confident that your child will also be able to discuss the record with you since we review notations after each session. The children are quite adept at "reading" these records.

Teachers at _____ Elementary School will be presenting an evening program for the P.T.A. We'll be discussing the running records and retelling process in detail. The information will provide background for understanding your child's record as well as tips for assisting your child with reading at home. We look forward to meeting lots of parents that night. Watch for this event in the P.T.A. newsletter.

Sincerely,

CHAPTER 2

Running-Record Warm-Ups

This chapter will guide you through the first step of getting ready to take running records—the initial stage that includes identifying particular behaviors, introducing the observation process to your class, capturing your observations in anecdotal notes, and thinking about how to use the information to support the reading development of your students. The rest of the chapter provides specific information on how to select an appropriate text for an oral-reading session, details on how to observe and record reading behaviors, and suggestions for how to share your observations with the reader. Finally, I will guide you through a session in which I observed a child's oral reading, took anecdotal notes, and then discussed my observations with him.

Kid Watching

"Kid watching" (Yetta Goodman, 1986), or learning how to watch closely and notice specific reading behaviors used by children, is an important first step. Instead of trying to mark each word and behavior, carefully observe the child as she reads, and make general notes on what you see. When reviewing notes, consider, "What does this specific behavior/word mean?"

Identify Behaviors.

When I first started to take running records, I felt jittery as I sat down with the reader. Although my professional training had included extensive practice in testing procedures with a wide range of instruments, this was new. The format was standard, but the text would be different for each reader. In addition, each child would bring his own history, strengths, and weaknesses.

The first goal I set for myself was to listen to children's oral reading with a focus on behaviors that are essential to fluency and comprehension. Appreciating that fluency, including automatic word recognition and a smooth flow throughout the reading, usually results in solid comprehension, I would take general notes based on the criteria listed in "What to Watch for While They Read Aloud" and "Examples of Notes on Observing a Child's Oral Reading." Overall performance, rather than individual errors, was my focus at that point.

Although I was nowhere near taking a full running record with all the symbols, there were notable benefits to starting in this gradual way.

❧ My students became familiar with the process and comfortable with the expectations.

❧ I had an opportunity to practice taking notes.

❧ I could verify immediate needs and use this to plan instruction.

❧ A positive tone was established for the steps that followed.

What to Watch for While They Read Aloud

As you observe a child during an oral-reading session, answer the following questions. Does the child:

❧ try to make overall sense of what he's reading?

❧ read smoothly so that the reading sounds like talking?

❧ use context (meaning or semantic) cues?

❧ read in meaningful phrases or chunks?

❧ make logical predictions about words he's uncertain of?

❧ use his knowledge of language patterns (syntactic cues—what kinds of words come next to sound the way we order words when we talk)?

❧ use his knowledge of letters and their associated sounds (graphophonemic, or visual, cues)?

❧ use confirmation and self-correction strategies?

❧ use the cues in an integrated (orchestrated) way?

❧ appear to be enjoying reading?

Adapted from ILEA/Center for Language in Primary Education (1989). *The Primary Language Record*. NH: Heinemann.

Tell Readers What You're Doing

From the beginning, enlist the children's help. Tell them what you're doing and why you're doing it, and show and explain your notes. Collaboration yields many benefits.

❋ When children understand what we're looking for, they'll try to reach that expectation.

❋ When they understand that our observations will help us help them grow as readers, they accept the assessment as a nonthreatening tool.

❋ When they receive specific feedback, sensitively delivered, readers are happy to focus on the behaviors we've discussed and self-monitor their performance.

I started by telling my first graders that I was learning something new and needed to practice. And I told them that I needed their patience and help.

With some of the other teachers, I've been learning how to listen to children as they read and notice the way they figure out words, read with expression, and remember what they've read. I'm going to watch how you do these things and practice writing about it while you're reading. When you're through, I'll tell you what my notes say, and you can let me know if I forgot anything.

The children made helping me a personal crusade, and in the process they helped themselves. Sharing my observations and notations initiated lively discussions. Children considered my insights and soon added their own comments, reactions, and even reasons for specific behaviors. They became metacognitive readers—more thoughtful while reading. Our discussions focused on skills and strategies taught previously in mini-lessons, and the children were more reflective about their overall performance. Children would comfortably tell me what I missed noting. They'd say: *Did you put down that I read in an excited voice for the exclamation mark? Did you put down that I went back to fix up that part when it didn't make sense?* They'd listen to what I told another child and say: *I read it like talking (chunking words), just like you said Billy did.*

This ice-breaking phase allowed me to be a risk taker. I didn't have to be perfect from the start. I could evolve as an efficient observer and recorder, and I had a collaborator (the reader) during each session. Admitting my novice status helped the children realize that learning is something everyone does—even adults. We all learned that learning is easier when we're not afraid to make mistakes and when we have friends who will help us.

When I got into trouble, I'd admit it and ask the children for their help.

You're reading right along, but I keep getting a little behind in my notes. You know the words, so if you slow down just a little—just a tad—it will be easier to chunk your words to sound more like talking or

Examples of Notes on Observing a Child's Oral Reading

❧ Was confident.

❧ Was interested.

❧ Maintained appropriate concentration on the task.

❧ Could identify the genre type for the selection (expository, narrative, poetry, for example).

❧ Created text (child was not really reading the print on the page, but was making up a story to accompany the pictures).

❧ Matched speech to print (child matched reading with words on the page, an important emergent behavior).

❧ Finger pointed to follow print.

❧ Tracked print visually (child could visually follow the print—left to right, return sweep to the next line—without using a finger or marker).

❧ Took initiative in attempting unknown words:

- Skipped to read on and returned to reread.
- Looked back for clue (i.e., in previously read section for meaning reference).
- Used semantic (meaning), syntactic (structure) or visual (letter/sound) clues.
- Used picture clues.
- Used personal speech pattern as an aid in decoding.
- Used background knowledge as an aid in decoding.
- Used beginning sounds, ending sounds, rhyming part (i.e., -at, -ake, -ook), and blended decoded parts together.
- Decoded longer words by syllables—recognizes root word and affix (i.e., look-ing—looking; un-happy—unhappy)—and blended parts.
- Could use combinations of the above strategies to decode smoothly, limiting interruptions in the overall flow of reading.

❧ Asked for help in a dependent way when didn't know or was unsure of a word.

❧ Self-corrected errors.

❧ Used prompts successfully.

❧ Read in meaningful units; chunked words to read phrases.

❧ Read smoothly, fluently—few hesitations or interruptions.

❧ Read expressively in appropriate places; used punctuation for meaning to enliven the text.

❧ Focused on meaning rather than word accuracy.

❧ Self-monitored about whether the reading was making sense.

❧ Focused on word accuracy rather than meaning.

❧ Balanced attention to accuracy and meaning processing.

❧ Summarized what was read satisfactorily.

❧ Commented and reacted to indicate comprehension and personal interpretations.

storytelling. Remember that's how we want it to sound. It'll also be easier for me to take notes.)

In their efforts to help me, their pacing improved. Racing through the text was replaced with reading in meaningful phrases.

Practice Taking Anecdotal Notes

Starting off with anecdotal notes that focused on efficient listening and note-taking, rather than taking a full record of the reading event, made the overall goal of taking a running record seem achievable. This manageable initial step built confidence and increased my powers of observation.

The perspectives that the children shared on their reading were often amazingly insightful. I could hear echoes (and paraphrasing) of my own comments. For example, a child might say: *I read that part again because it didn't sound right with the story. The repeat sounded more like it would if I was [talking] saying it or telling someone else.*

The children also developed empathy for me as the observer/recorder when they tried taking anecdotal notes on each other's reading during free time. After observing others, junior recorders became more adept at applying fix-up strategies themselves. The children became supportive cheerleaders of one another's progress. Beyond literacy skills, they were building their classroom community. Here's how one first grader responded to his classmate Billy's reading:

Billy fix a wrd he sad it lod for the ! good jb	(Billy fixed a word. He said it loud for the surprise mark. Good job.)

Practice Using Anecdotal Notes

My initial efforts at taking anecdotal notes before taking full running records became a learning experience for the class. Everyone participated in noticing and noting growth in one another and themselves. Sometimes I'd plan a mini-lesson around a new skill and sometimes around a skill the children were already using, but confusing. Children's records, as well as my own, guided further instruction. Observing learners made me aware of the most effective sequence for introducing and reinforcing the skills and strategies outlined in district requirements. I always let the children know when I built mini-lessons on their observations. For example, a mini-lesson on using the analogy method to decode words came out of discussions with children as I took anecdotal notes.

As the children listened to each other, they began to take note of strategies I'd emphasized in mini-lessons. For example, Stephanie, who was quite

Using Known Words to Figure Out New Words

Time: 10 minutes, following a recording of daily news

Materials: News of the day (or use any type of morning message content you favor)

Objective: To introduce children to the analogy method for decoding words and give them an opportunity to practice it with word families found in the "daily news" and words in their speaking vocabulary

Motivation: T: Sometimes it must seem like there are so many words to figure out. But you know what? There are lots of clues you can use to make it easier. Thinking about what the story is all about is the best place to start. Today I'll show you how you can use words you know to figure out new words.

Teacher Modeling: T: First, thinking of what would make sense and sound right helps your brain come up with ideas. Then you have to decide which sensible word is the word in front of you. Looking at "hunks and chunks" of words makes knowing it quicker. That's important when you're reading because you don't want to forget what's happening in the story. In the news today—in Melissa's sentence—if I didn't know the word *clown*, I'd think about who would come to a birthday party and make those twisty balloons for everyone. If I still didn't know the word, I'd look at it and think it has a part like the color word *brown*. I just have to put a different beginning on it, a c-l, /cl/ with the /own/ part and "presto bingo!" I've got *clown*. And that makes sense in her sentence because she was talking about a clown who came to the birthday party and made twisty balloons for everyone. Clowns do that.

Let's try to think of other words we can make with the /own/ part.

Guided Practice: T: How would you finish the sentence, If I said, "The animal musicians were on their way to Bremen _____ (blank)."

C: *Town.* Like The Bremen Town Musicians in the story.

T: How would *town* look? What would spell the /t/ part and what would spell the /own/ part?

C: T and OWN.

T: Tommy, will you write town right here?

T: If I make a face like this, people would call my expression the word I'll write right here. (I slowly wrote the word *frown*.) Who can read this word?

C: /fr—/own/ Oh, it's *frown*. That's what they call a sad face.

Independent Practice: T: When you're reading today and come to a word you don't know, I want you to think about what the sentence is all about. Use word chunks that are just like parts of other words you know to figure it out. When you're writing in your journals and are trying to spell a new word, compare parts you hear in it to chunks that sound the same in a word you already know how to spell.

Closure: T: Who can explain the strategy we learned today?

C: When I don't know a word I come to, I can think about what's happening or reread to remember what's happening. If I still don't know it, I can look for word parts in it that are like parts of words I know. Then you just have to change the beginning or ending and make the new word. It's like my Transformers when I turn them into something else.

C: You can use word parts to spell too. Then you spell a bigger part at a time instead of one letter, then one letter, then one letter—like that.

Evaluation: I observed children's comments and responses during the lesson as well as their independent use of the skill in everyday reading and writing activities. I determined their level of competence with it. Further class, small group, and individual reinforcement was necessary.

an accomplished observer, listened and recorded her observations as Jenny read and worked on the strategy of using known words to figure out new words. When Stephanie shared her anecdotal notes, we talked about how clever Jenny was to use sound comparison and picture clues to figure out an unknown word.

Jenny got mixd up on brake for the bik. She red it gin and siad its lik make with a ake part. Then she siad O, it's the brake for the bik It's the hndl br kind	Jenny got mixed up on brake for the bike. She read it again and said it's like "make" with an -ake part. Then she said, "Oh, it's the brake for the bike. It's the handlebar kind."

Practice is the key to developing proficiency with anecdotal notes and readiness for the next step. To complete the initial work of getting ready to take full running records, take anecdotal notes on each of your student's oral reading. This will give you 20–30 practice sessions with the note-taking process. Set up a schedule that will work in your classroom for these observations. If you meet with one or two children a day while the others engage in independent work, you'll probably be able to complete a session with everyone in two to four weeks. Give yourself enough time to develop fluency and comfort with each step along the way to taking full running records.

How to Match a Student With a Reading Selection

Selecting an appropriate text for the oral-reading session is critically important. The book or selection should be challenging, but not overwhelming for the reader. It should be a text at the child's instructional level (see "Make the Text Fit the Reader," Chapter 1, page 14 for an explanation of levels)—one that will require her to apply known reading strategies independently. Books at the frustrational level are too difficult for a reader to use known strategies. Independent-level books, where the child knows most or all of the words, are too easy. Easy books are appropriate for independent silent-reading time.

Introduce children to the idea of different reading levels and discuss how levels vary for individuals and are constantly changing as readers grow. Explain that a book that is independent, or too easy, for one person may be instructional, or just right, for another at this time. Help the students classify a text's reading level for themselves using the Goldilocks test (see page 27).

A 10-Step Anecdotal Note-Taking Plan

1 Tell the children what will be happening during the oral-reading sessions and why. Explain that while you and individual students work together, the rest of the class will work independently. Go over any ground rules for acceptable activities and behaviors.

2 Post a weekly schedule of the reading conferences in a central location in the room. Start with one per day. After a few weeks, you may feel that you can complete two per day.

3 Invite each reader to join you in a quiet area of the room. Have him bring a book that matches the Goldilocks "just-right" category. It may be a book the class is reading for its literature studies, a book the child has been reading, or a book you've read to the class. Most important, it must offer some, but not too much, challenge.

4 While the child reads the book aloud, take notes using the reading behavior and strategy guides. (See "Examples of Notes on Observing a Child's Oral Reading," page 22.) Focus on what the reader says and does. You'll add interpretations and comments later.

5 Talk briefly with the child about the book's content (a retell) to be sure he has comprehended it.

6 Discuss the notes you took while the child read. Encourage him to comment on your observations and add any of his own.

7 As soon as possible, revisit the anecdotal notes you took during the session and during your post-reading conversations with the child. Add any thoughts and conclusions about the child's performance.

8 Plan weekly meetings with one or more colleagues, including resource teachers. Share your anecdotal notes, and invite reactions and alternative interpretations. The following questions will guide your discussions and stimulate conversation:

   ❖ Was the child comfortable and confident?

   ❖ Did she understand what she read? Fully or just the gist of it? Where was the confusion?

   ❖ Did many errors cause the meaning to be lost? What caused the errors?

   ❖ Did she make connections with background knowledge and earlier reading?

   ❖ Did she read smoothly? How accurately did she read words?

   ❖ Did she use multiple clues (cues) to figure out words? What were they?

   ❖ Did she attempt to self-correct? What strategies did she use? How successful was she?

9 Add insights from meetings with colleagues to your notes. File your notes and reports in the children's portfolios.

10 Follow this plan until you've completed anecdotal notes on one session with each child.

The Goldilocks (and the Three Bears) Test
Choose a "Just-Right" Book to Read to the Teacher

Too Easy—My independent level

I know all or most of the words in the book or on a page.

I know a lot about this topic.

I've read the book many times before.

Just Right—My instructional level

The book looks interesting, and I know something about the topic.

I know most of the words in the book or on a page.

There's someone to help me when I need it.

Too Hard—My frustrational level

There are a lot of words I don't know.

I don't know a lot about this topic.

There's no one to read this book to me.

Adapted from Ohlausen and Jepsen, 1992, as cited in Tompkins, 1998

When you're figuring out levels with the class, or with a child individually, you can use the fingers-up method. As they skim through a book, have the children note the number of words they don't know on a page or in a paragraph by putting up a finger for each. If four or five fingers go up, the book is probably too hard (frustrational) right now. If two or three go up, it's probably just right (instructional). And if zero to one go up, it's probably too easy (independent). Children quickly catch on to this technique, and the self-analysis builds metacognitive skills.

It's important to emphasize to the children that learning and practicing new skills are key ingredients in reading growth. I use sports as an analogy. I tell the children how coaches teach new plays, and players practice them over and over again in training, in scrimmages, and in real games. Like the baseball player who works to improve his batting average, the reader has the power to improve his reading level. The rate of change for the player—and the reader—is based on how much time is given to practicing skills and strategies.

Before children read aloud for an assessment, I ask them to select a book that has some hard words in it (instructional level). It may be a book that they've heard or read before. I tell them that I need to see what strategies they use when they meet a word that they don't know right away. This will help me plan my teaching. The children use the Goldilocks test and guesstimate with the fingers-up technique what will be a "just-right" book.

They also use the Goldilocks test to select books for independent reading or D.E.A.R. time.

Sometimes the book or passage a child chooses for oral reading turns out to be at his independent level. That can be a pleasant surprise. Celebrate the growth—the pants are too short!

Wow, you did a fantastic job on that book! I can tell you've been reading up a storm and getting lots of practice. It's too easy for reading out loud to me. Let's find another one with a Goldilocks fit—not too hard and not too easy.

TEACHING TIP
. . . .
Let Interest Lead the Way

Interest and motivation can have a powerful effect on what a child reads—regardless of level. When a child is determined to read a certain book because he wants to know what's in it, he'll read it with a level of comprehension that satisfies his personal curiosity. He'll find the support needed to navigate the text. He may work more slowly, but he'll absorb the content because he needs the information or badly wants to know the story. A book can lead a child's reading development.

Observing and Recording How the Reader Uses Skills and Strategies

Now you're ready to begin your scheduled oral-reading assessments. Explain to the class that you'll be listening to a reader today during their D.E.A.R. time. Ask that child to select a just-right book that she would like to read to you. Sit in a comfortable area of the room that is relatively free of distractions. Review what you'd like the reader to do, the purpose, and what you'll be doing. Remind her that you'll be taking notes and that after she's through, you'll let her see the notes. Show her the form you'll be writing on (see the blank form on page 33), explaining that *familiar* means she's seen or heard it before and *unfamiliar* means she hasn't. Then reassure her that, together, you and she will be talking about the strategies she used to figure out words

Following along as the child reads, use phrases and bulleted points to take general notes. Use "What to Watch for While They Read Aloud", page 20, and "Examples of Notes on Observing a Child's Oral Reading," page 22, as guides for making meaningful observations and reports on the child's performance. Keep your notes clear, yet concise. Focus on the child's performance. You can make additional comments after you share your notes with the child. Be sure to do this as soon as possible, before your memory fades.

As she reads, keep the child focused on the task at hand. Here are two ways I keep the reader on track:

If the reader stops, makes no attempt to try an unknown word, and instantly appeals for help, I prompt her to think about how to figure it out:

What can you do? What's a first step?

If the response is silence, I suggest:

Read on and come back to this. See if more information and sounds you know for the letters you see help you figure it out.

If the reader makes a miscue (mistake) that doesn't make any sense and continues on, I usually interrupt the reading:

It sounded like you just said, "Tommy and Sam ran into the horse." Does that sound right to you?

Most often I'll get a *no* head nod, so I direct and guide the reader through the fix-up process.

Let's go back and look at that again. Remember, it started to rain when they were camping in the backyard. Where would they go to get out of the rain? It has to start with /h/ because that's the beginning sound of the word in that place—into the /h/.

If the child comes up with *house*, I congratulate her. I talk about how the letters on the page and sounds for these—*h*-/h/, *ou*-/ou/, and *s*-/s/— spell out a word that makes sense in the story. The word can't be *horse* because that doesn't make any sense. I explain that even though the word *cabin* would make sense, it couldn't be *cabin* because that isn't an *h* word.

Emphasizing to children that reading must make sense is critically important. Good readers use fix-up strategies when the meaning is lost; otherwise, comprehension is seriously interrupted as the reader continues. Talking about and modeling strategies may not be enough. The reader's first attempts at applying them in context need to be scaffolded (guided)— some more than others.

If the reader's miscue makes sense in the context, I don't interrupt the reading. However, when the child has finished, I selectively go back to one (or two) of these as a teaching point.

You read, "Most woodlands are dominated by one kind of tree, such as oak or maple." Let's look at that part again—Most woodlands are dominated by one t-y-p-e of tree. Kind made sense in the sentence, but the author's word doesn't start with /k/. That was a good substitution for the word if you didn't know it. By reading on you were able to keep thinking about the information. That was a good strategy. Now, let's look closer at

Tom and the Beanstalk— A Tale of One Oral-Reading Session

For his oral reading session, Tom chose Steven Kellogg's version of *Jack and the Beanstalk,* a book he'd read many times but that was still at the instructional level for him. While he read, I took anecdotal notes. After he read and before we discussed my notes, I talked briefly with Tom about the content of the book (a general retelling) to evaluate his comprehension. (Chapter 4 will go into detail on structured retelling.) Then I shared my anecdotal notes with him (see right).

Oral Reading Anecdotal Notes Assessment Form

Name ___Tom___   Date __11/15/__

Book read __Jack and the Beanstalk – S. Kellogg__

Familiar/Unfamiliar __Familiar__

_____ Teacher-selected   ___✓___ Student-selected

Comments:

- excited about reading this book
- "chunking" is much better – he's reading phrases
- attempts at expression – not always appropriate or matching punctuation
- reread for clarity
- self corrected – mostly omissions
- substitutions made sense
  i.e. dummy for dolt
- mispronounced ogre as ō-grē, ŏg-rē, ō-grə – unfamiliar word (meaning)
- discussion focused on what was new or different in Kellogg's version
- noticed little man looked like a wizard – used this to establish time setting

Taking Running Records Scholastic Professional Books   33

Make the Retell Meaningful

Try to let the reader initiate the retell conversation. Or use a minimal prompt to get him started. Make this a literary exchange rather than a yes/no question-and-answer session. Move the discussion from summarizing to interpretative levels that tie text information with the child's background knowledge. For example, my post-reading retell conversation with Tom went something like this:

Teacher: What did you think of this story?

Tom: I liked this version because I like Steven Kellogg's pictures.

Teacher: What is it you like about them?

Tom: His characters always have the same look. Like Jack and Pecos Bill and Johnny Appleseed. They have faces like ordinary kids. It makes them seem real.

Teacher: Do you like Steven Kellogg's version of this story?

Tom: I like that the man who trades for the beans is like a wizard in the time of kings and queens and knights. He's not like that in other books I've seen.

Teacher: Did you notice any other differences?

Tom: I like the part with the giant—the ŏg-r ē. (Tom mispronounces the word.)

Teacher: The ō-ger? (I respond with the pronunciation.)

Tom: Yeah. He's not just a giant, like a huge person. He's a creature! His wife kind of helped Jack, but he lied to her.

Teacher: What did you think of the way Jack treated the ogre?

Tom: The ogre was scary, but Jack was in his house when he didn't like kids. Jack stole from him and that's not right. I think Jack was greedy. You can't steal from people's houses. Jack should get in trouble.

How I Discussed My Notes With Tom

Teacher: I wrote down that you used chunking and read in phrases instead of one word at a time. You've been working hard on that, and it showed here. You made it sound like storytelling.

Tom: I wanted to sound like the story reader who visited our class last week. Everybody liked to listen to him read with different voices.

Teacher: I wrote that you tried to use expression, especially when you read the character parts. There is a lot of character talking in this book. You have to keep changing from one to the other as you read. The punctuation marks and how we think the character must feel help us decide how to say the words. How did you know when to change your voice?

Tom: On this page, where Jack's mother threw the beans out the window, I knew she was mad. Her face shows it. Jack gave the cow away for beans, and that's not enough to eat. There are two exclamation marks—here and here—so you're supposed to read these words with emotion.

Teacher: Steven Kellogg calls the giant an *ogre*. That means a man-eating giant. Isn't that a perfect word for this character?

Tom: I never knew it before, but it sounds like a nasty creature.

Teacher: Jack's mother asked him how he could have acted like a *dolt*. This word—right here—is *dolt*. It means "like a silly person." You were close when you substituted *dummy*.

Good thinking! I can tell you're comparing Kellogg's version to one in your head. You've noticed some interesting differences. You helped me understand why you really like this book.

Tom: It's my favorite book. He tells the story the best and draws neat pictures.

Teacher: Keep working on chunking words. Practice that and reading with expression, especially when buddy reading. Your partner can tell you if it sounds smooth—like storytelling.

I enjoyed listening to you. I could tell you were excited about sharing this book. Is there something else you did well today that I didn't write down?

Tom: I didn't need a lot of help today.

Teacher: That's right. You read right along and even made self-corrections when you got confused. Good observation.

I'll let you take Sam's place at the center and ask him to come over to read now. Thanks, Tom.

At a later time, when students are working independently or during my planning period, I compare notes taken on this reading with those of previous ones. I note patterns, areas of growth (i.e., improvement in smoothness, meaningful substitutions) and specific needs (i.e., attention to punctuation) that I will set as instructional objectives.

For Tom, I wrote:

> *Tom's fluency has improved. He reads along without stumbling or hesitating—seems to trust his decoding ability. He used to expect problems.*
>
> *He's putting in a meaningful synonym when he can't figure out a word. He's holding onto meaning, but he's not trying to decode the text word first. We've got to work on this. He's missing chances to improve decoding skills and increase his vocabulary.*
>
> *He really enjoyed this book. He attends to illustrations. He has a fine-tuned artistic sense!*

Close attention to young readers' developing literacy achievement allows us to shape their learning. Sharing our observations with readers stimulates them to recognize their own progress and become personally involved in setting appropriate goals. Children begin to take control of their reading.

The running-record warm-ups have established your observational and reporting abilities. You can now easily identify important reading behaviors, efficiently document them, discuss them with students, and use your observations to establish future instructional goals.

Both you and your students now feel comfortable with the format and are ready to move on to the next step toward a complete running record.

Oral Reading Anecdotal Notes Assessment Form

Name_____ Date _____

Book read_____

Familiar/Unfamiliar_____

_____ Teacher-selected   _____ Student-selected

Comments:

_____

_____

_____

_____

_____

_____

_____

_____

_____

_____

_____

_____

_____

_____

_____

CHAPTER 3

Taking a Running Record

Ms. Murray takes a running record with Anna Maria.

You've spent several weeks taking anecdotal notes on reading behaviors in a formalized way. You've discussed your observations with the children, and you've documented these observations for analysis, instructional planning, and reporting on performance. Now you're ready for the next step—creating a detailed running record of a child's reading of each word. Was the word read correctly or was there an error? What kind of error was it? For me, a running record is truly the most efficient and effective reading assessment tool, and I'm forever grateful to Marie Clay for devising it. Without this detailed evidence, small nuances of change can easily go unnoticed and, therefore, cannot be considered in planning the next steps for instruction. Through coding a running record, we gather significant information on how well a child reads words (*text processing*). Through the child's retelling of what he has read, which comes immediately after the reading, we learn how well he understands what he reads (*meaning processing*).

The full RR procedure includes information on both text and meaning processing. This chapter focuses on the accuracy of the child's reading of the word. I've addressed the procedures for retelling in the next chapter.

Getting Up to Speed

While the mechanics of taking a running record may seem overwhelming at first, do not despair. The shorthand marks, or codes, introduced here will help you to quickly record all the details you notice, capturing an entire reading episode for later analysis. Soon the marks will become second nature, and you'll find that you're able to keep up with even a fluent reader. Though it takes time and practice for the markings to become automatic, the benefit to your teaching is immeasurable. So get ready to dive in!

Start Off Using Tapes

I believe that tape recording or videotaping the reader is essential when you're starting to use running-records. Using the tape, you can continue to focus on general note taking during the reading and create the running-record from the tape later. Gradually, you can start using the running-record codes as the child reads and use the tape to verify and clarify the markings. Over time, you'll find fewer and fewer differences between your initial running-record and the tape. Once the tapes validate your records, you've become an expert! You may want to continue making tapes, but you won't need to rely on them. (You may even want to use the tapes during a parent teacher conference)

TEACHING TIP

Tape Oral Readings and Reap Extra Rewards

✤ Kids love seeing and hearing their tapes. They're eager to reread the text as they watch, listen, and identify and analyze their own errors. I've heard comments like: *I knew I said that! Listen to this next part, coming up. I say the wrong word and it sounds crazy when I get to the end. So I go back and fix it, and I get it!* Some children even perform better for the camera; they're on stage—front and center—and inject every word with passion and expression. Children also love to listen to their tapes individually or with peers at learning centers. Partners' discussions are rich with observations and talk of how to use strategies.

✤ Parents love it too. When you show parents how their child reads and they actually witness her literacy development, they become strong advocates for your program. They also understand the difficulties their child may be having with the reading process and become more supportive of early intervention programs.

Be Flexible About Word Length

The length of texts the children choose to read can vary. Though I generally keep 100 words as an approximate lower limit, passages will be shorter for students at the emergent level. Allow children to go beyond 100 words and even complete a story or text when they're really involved and on a roll. Fluency and comprehension naturally improve as readers begin to grasp the overall gist of a text. If the text is a picture book and the reader appears to be comfortable, let him finish it. With chapter books, stop at an appropriate pause in the action.

A List of Running Record Codes

(Adapted from Clay, 1993; Goodman & Burke, 1972; Johns, 1993; Leslie & Caldwell, 1990)

Use the following codes and procedures to record a student's text-processing behaviors. I've included scoring guidelines for each procedure, but I'll illustrate how scoring works in more detail later in the chapter.

1. Correct word: Use a check mark.

Mark every word read accurately with a check. The checks must match the number of words in each line of text. Record page (or paragraph) numbers for later reference. The record should match the text—line by line, page by page.	Page 1 Sometimes it looked ✓✓✓ like spilt milk. ✓✓✓ But it wasn't spilt milk. ✓✓✓✓ From "It Looked Like Spilt Milk" by Charles Shaw

2. Incorrect word (miscue): Record the incorrect word the reader said with the text word under it. These are also called substitution miscues.

Score incorrect words as errors.	reader: horse text: house

3. Trials/attempts: Record each incorrect attempt above the correct word.

Sounding out may be recorded in lower case letters, (c-a-t). **Score unsuccessful attempts as errors.**	reader horse—h..h..h—home text: house

4. Reader's self-corrections: Mark as **sc**. Record each self-correction by crossing out the miscue and writing the letters **sc** above it.

When scoring, these are figured into the self-correction frequency but not the accuracy percent.	reader: ~~when~~ sc text: where

5. Word omission: Record an empty circle above the text word or write down the omitted text word and circle it.

Score the omitted word as an error.	reader: ◯ or (green)
	text: green

6. Word insertion: Record any inserted word by writing it above a caret.

Score insertions as errors.	the
	∧

7. Teacher-given word: Insert **T**, which stands for *told*.

If the teacher tells the reader the word because child is stuck, it is marked with a **T**. The teacher might first suggest, *Try the strategies you know to figure it out* (i.e., clunk strategies). **Score T words as errors.**	reader: horse
	text: house — T

8. Appeal for help: Write **A** when the child appeals for help. Write the miscue made if the child makes an attempt when prompted to try. Record **T** if the word is then teacher-given.

When the reader asks for help, the teacher suggests: *You try it. Use the strategies you know.* Then the teacher can observe the reader's ability to apply strategies taught and practiced. If the child is still unsuccessful, the word is teacher-given (**T**). **Score words given as errors.**	reader: — A — horse
	text: house T

9. Start over: Record **SO** with the repeated text in a bracket.

If the reader seems to be totally confused and is making a series of errors, stop him and suggest that he start over. Show him where to begin again. The repeated text may be more than one line. **Score the start over as one error. Any corrections made are then scored as self-corrections.**

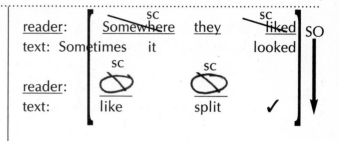

10. Repetition: Write ⟵——— **R** to indicate a repetition.

Repetitions often result in self-corrections. If the child repeats the same words several times, a sub number tells how many. The arrow is drawn back to the beginning of the repetition. If many repetitions are interrupting fluency and inhibiting comprehension, that should be noted in overall comments on the reading. **Do not count repetitions as errors.**

Examples:

text: Sometimes it looked   ✓✓✓

⟵———————R

text: The children ran to the new swings in the playground.

✓✓✓✓   ⊘ (new) sc   ✓

⟵———————R₂

✓✓✓

11. Hesitation: Write **H** to indicate a hesitation in decoding.

Mark a significant hesitation (3–4 seconds). It reflects choppy reading and a need for closer analysis in word recognition. Readers sometimes hesitate when they're anticipating difficulty with an upcoming word. They may be rereading silently to get a running start at the suspected unknown word.
A hesitation doesn't count as an error.

text: The tail is especially long.

✓✓✓ H - es... ✓   ✓
     especially

12. Reverse word order: Use a loop [⌒‿] to identify words reversed.

Sometimes readers reverse the order of words in the text. Often they are following a previous pattern in the text or a familiar pattern of speech, and the reversal does not interrupt meaning. **Score reversals as two errors—one for each word.**	You can ride along with me again any time you want, said Dad. ✓✓✓✓✓✓ ✓✓✓ said Dad ‿

13. Attempts with partial result or nonword: Record the attempt above the correct text word.

A reader may attempt a word but come up with a partial word or nonword. It's important to record what the attempt is. This reveals word and letter/sound knowledge as well as strategies that the reader is trying. **Score incorrect attempts as errors.**	reader: text:	disappoint disappointment	dipidnend depended

14. Variations on the text word: Record the reader's spoken word over the correct text word.

The reader may make an error involving a sound, grammatical, or vocabulary variation resulting from regional, cultural, or dialectical differences. Or he may pronounce a word incorrectly because of difficulty with articulation. **Dialectical miscues should not be counted as oral-reading errors unless the teacher knows the student pronounces the word in the standard form in other situations.**	reader: text:	mus must	wuv love

15. Changing the correct word to an incorrect one: Record a slash through the check mark for that word, and write the miscue above it.

Sometimes readers abandon the correct reading of a word and reread it incorrectly. When reviewing the record with the reader, explore why the change was made—what thoughts went through the reader's mind. **This change is scored as an error.**	It was probably a mistake. possibly ✓ ✓ ✗ ✓ ✓ probably

16. Pronunciation shift: Record the word as the child pronounced it (showing his emphasis and how the meaning was changed) above the text word.

When reviewing the record with the reader, find out if he knew the meaning of the desired word, but simply used the incorrect pronunciation. **Pronunciation shifts that change the word count as errors.**	reader: rec ´ ord (an account) text: re cord´ (to note)

17. Teacher prompt: P, plus individual codes showing a teacher-suggested strategy. If the reader gets the word, it is marked with a **P** (which notes what kind of prompt it was) and a check. If the reader misses the word, it is scored as an error. If the teacher has to provide the word, it is marked either **A-T** (appeal, then teacher-given) or **T** (teacher-given with no appeal).

Teacher-prompted strategy codes	What the teacher suggested to the reader
P-cc	Try context clues
P-pc	Try picture clues
P-sc	Try letter/sound clues

If the reader appeals for help but isn't ready to use word identification strategies independently, the teacher may prompt the child to use a certain strategy (see above).

This intervention allows the teacher to determine that the child knows strategies and how to apply them but is unable to initiate them or decide which would be most efficient in the particular situation.

If the accuracy score is within the independent range but several prompts were given, the text may still be at the reader's instructional level.

Examples:

She worked at the library after

✓✓✓ A P-pc✓ ✓
library

school. ✓

The spaceship landed right in

H P-pc sc

✓ ⬭ ✓✓✓
space

←————————R

front of his house. ✓✓✓✓

I have used these prompting codes effectively with running records, but they are not found in traditional running records or Informal Reading Inventories (IRIs).

18. **Punctuation omissions:** There are differences of opinion regarding the scoring of punctuation omissions. Leslie & Caldwell (1990) do not count repetitions, hesitations, and omissions of punctuation because they tend to be scored unreliably. Johns (1993) recommends that the teacher count the omission of words and punctuation in a tally of total miscues. Punctuation errors should be noted. The degree to which they interrupt fluency and appear to inhibit efficient comprehension should also be noted.

19. **Print conventions:** With emergent readers, note directional movement on the page (left page first, left to right –L to R–, return sweep, top to bottom –T to B–), tracking of the print, and accuracy in one-to-one word matching. This can be done with symbols (←———, ———➤), letters (L to R, T to B) and words.

Becoming Code Savvy

In order to get comfortable using the RR codes, you'll want to start slowly. With practice you'll pick up speed. Here are two ways to practice before you record, while actually sitting with children as they read:

1 **Listen and think.** Throughout the day—in literature study, social studies, science, or during any lesson in which children are taking turns reading aloud—watch for reading errors. Make mental notes. For example, while the student is reading aloud, think to yourself: *Tom skipped the word* light. *That was an omission. I'd use the circle. Now, he made a substitution. He said* dark forest *instead of* dense *forest. I'd write* dark *above a line and go back later to fill in* dense.

2 **Listen and code.** Have individual children read predetermined literature selections into a tape recorder during independent-work time. They love it, and they enjoy making comments to you as they read into the tape recorder. *How'd ya like that, Mrs. Shea. I did it real good—all by myself. I liked this story, and I know why the dinosaur's a dirty rotten cheater. I'll whisper my idea to you at snack time. I'm done. I'll get Danny to read it next.* I often find myself chuckling as I listen to student's recordings, and I try to respond to their comments and questions as soon as possible.

Practice with coding by taking the tapes home and, following along with the particular text, writing the markings on a running record form (copy the blank form on pages 62–63 or use a sheet of blank paper). You can rewind the tape as often as necessary. This process gives you a chance to collect a lot of samples in a few days. You can practice with colleagues, comparing markings and checking one another.

My students enjoyed recording their reading and listening to their tapes so much that I made it an ongoing option in a learning center. They'd listen, note their errors, and decide to redo the reading to improve accuracy, expression, and fluency. Research on the value of repeated reading for improving fluency and comprehension supports this highly motivating practice (Walker, 1996).

The Main Event

Now you're ready to begin using running-record codes as students read. You're sitting next to the reader with a copy—or a shared copy—of the text and a running record form or a piece of blank paper. You have a clipboard to help you write quickly and efficiently. The tape recorder is ready. Don't panic about getting everything right. You're going to treat this first write-up of the oral reading as a draft and revise it after listening to the tape recording. Your confidence and proficiency will develop with practice.

Before you have the child begin reading, there are two more things to do: introduce the new procedures—the tape recording and coding—and determine, or supplement, the child's prior knowledge (*schema*) on the topic of the text.

Introducing What's New

The children will need to understand what you'll be doing next so curiosity about it doesn't distract them as they read. My explanation goes something like this:

> *Today I'm going to have you read aloud from a book like we've done before, but there's something new. The tape recorder will be on so that I can record your reading and listen to it again later. I'll let you listen to it too—a little bit after we finish and all of it by yourself at the listening center tomorrow. Something else new: I'll be making a mark for each word you say—to keep the place and remember what you've done. Let's look at the marks together now so you'll know what they mean.*
>
> *The next part is the same as before. After you finish reading, I want you to tell me all about what you've read, as if I were someone who had never heard it before—tell what happened and what you think about it. So, think about what the author is saying as you read. If you meet any words that are hard for you, use the strategies you know to figure them out. Let's think a minute about those. Can you tell me what you'd do to figure out a word? (I review word-recognition strategies I've taught.)*
>
> *If you don't have any trouble, we'll know that you've grown so much as a reader that this book is too easy for you. I'll ask you to read a harder book, so I can see what you do when you have to use strategies to figure out words. That will show me how I can help you grow even more as a reader.*

After I've introduced the new procedures to the student and answered any questions he may have, I don't need to restate these. I do continue to review decoding strategies with students who may not be fully independent with them. And I always remind readers that they'll be asked to retell the passage.

Children soon become very comfortable with the overall procedure and fully understand the meanings associated with different marks. They're also

Use Shorthand to Help You Keep Up

If a reader hasn't made any further miscues on a line and has moved onto the next, use a dash to indicate that more checks are needed on that line for a count of total words. Go onto the next line with the reader, then count the words and fill in the checks later.

line	TEXT	CODES
1	Plants provide the basic food for life	✓✓✓ ~~best~~^{SC} _____ basic
2	in the ocean, just as they do on land.	✓✓✓✓✓✓✓
3	Plants that grow underwater are called	✓✓✓ under^{SC}_____ ~~the~~^{SC} ~~water~~^{SC}____ underwater ^ ^
4	algae, and there are two main groups	✓✓✓✓✓✓
5	found in the oceans.	✓✓✓✓
	From *Life in the Oceans* by Lucy Baker, pg. 10	

LATER

Line 1: Three more checks are added for the words *food, for,* and *life*

Line 3: Two checks are added for the words *are* and *called*

When you're first using the running-record sheet, it may be difficult to record all miscues. Focus on getting down the child's words when a substitution or addition is offered and write in the correct (text) words later. It's easy enough to retrace the record and add the text words, but unless the reading is taped, the child's words and attempts at a word might be forgotten or only partially recalled. Page, line, or paragraph numbers will help you find your place when you're going back.

line	TEXT	CODES
1	Many marine animals spend their	✓ many ✓✓✓
2	entire lives sifting the water for	✓✓ ~~sitting~~^{SC} ✓✓✓ ←———R
3	plankton, but they in turn are hunted	✓✓✓✓✓✓
4	by other animals. It is estimated that for	✓✓✓✓ es...estimate ✓✓
5	every ten plankton-feeders at least	✓✓✓✓✓
6	one hunter lurks nearby.	✓✓✓
	From *Life in the Oceans* by Lucy Baker, pg. 14	

LATER

Line 1: I fill in *marine* below many.

Line 2: The child first reads *sitting* for *sifting*, then rereads, starting with his self-correction and moving forward. I fill in the word *sifting* under *sitting*.

Line 4: The child struggles over the word, attempts it, and almost gets it. **I want to record each utterance of the attempt. Such efforts reveal decoding competence.** I fill in the word *estimated* under *estimate*.

quick to tell you if they think you've made a mistake. For example, once I had written a dash to remind myself to recount the words in a line that was free of errors, so that I could add the checks later but still keep up with the reader. The child was so adept at reading and watching me record that he commented, *I get three more checks there.* I assured him I would add the checks and explained how and why I used a special shorthand sometimes.

Finding Out What the Reader Already Knows

Have a conversation about the content of the text the child will be reading. Ask questions that will get him thinking, and take a "Picture Walk" through some of the illustrations. This preview of the selection enables the reader to make predictions about what's coming up and introduces the selection's vocabulary. If illustrations aren't available, give a brief prereading explanation about the topic to set the stage for reading. You might want to note key points of your conversation in the Comments section on the running record form (see page 62) or on your retelling sheet (i.e., *Jamie knows a lot about shadows—relying on prior knowledge*).

Comparing the reader's performance on topics she knows a lot about and those she knows little about can help guide your future instructional planning. Research shows that readers do much better when they think about what they already know about a topic or are given some background knowledge on the topic before they read. Some readers will always need more preparation than others. Record your overall determination of the child's schema on the topic of the selection based on your conversation with her.

Now turn on the tape recorder, and as the child reads, use the coding system to record everything he says and does. Observe strategies the child uses and his overall demeanor during the session (see Examples of Notes on Observing a Child's Oral Reading", Chapter 2, page 22). Make extra notes on the record as appropriate; the more details the better. Use the shorthand techniques so you can fill in text words and add checks for correct words later during a teacher preparation period or while the children are working independently. Remember that you'll get back to these records as soon as possible while the session is still fresh in your mind.

A structured retelling (see Chapter 4 for detailed guidelines) should immediately follow the oral-reading session. However, for now, as you're getting your feet wet, engage the reader in a general retelling about the passage to assess comprehension, make observations, and deliver feedback on the overall performance. Then share your markings, observations, and anecdotal notes on the retelling. Discuss particular miscues and self-corrections to make a few teaching points. Stress the successful reading behaviors you observed and collaboratively establish goals to work on.

Following the interaction with the reader, you'll want to review your markings and anecdotal notes. At this time, add information to clarify and extend comments you made on observations. Now, you're ready to do a detailed analysis of your coding for the text-processing part of the oral reading phase.

Keeping Score

Study the following running record (the errors are numbered and circled) of a child's reading from *Arthur Writes a Story* by Marc Brown. A step-by-step explanation for scoring accompanies it. Please note that the book text is shown on the running record form so you can learn the markings, you won't have to type it when actually taking a running record!

You'll want to take three kinds of calculations into consideration: accuracy (as shown in the Arthur example), error-frequency rate, and self-correction frequency rate.

Accuracy

Compute the accuracy rate to find the percentage of words the reader read correctly. This figure helps you determine a child's reading levels and is a key component in evaluating her overall reading ability. To compute word-reading accuracy, simply divide the number of words read correctly (the number of words in the selection minus the number of errors) by the total number of words in the selection. This gives a measure of word recognition competency.

Example: If the text had a total of 182 words and the child made 7 errors, I'd calculate that 175 words were read correctly (182-7=175). Then I'd compute the percent of accuracy by dividing 175 by 182: $\frac{175}{182} = 96\%$ accuracy.

Levels Attained on the Running Record

Easy (Independent)	**1.** % of accuracy (word recognition)	= 95% or higher
	2. Comprehension	= full/complete = 90%-100% if questions are used to score
Instructional	**1.** % of accuracy	= 90% or higher
	2. comprehension	= partial, but satisfactory = 75%-89% if questions are used to score
Hard (Frustrational)	**1.** % of accuracy	= below 90%
	2. comprehension	= fragmented = less than 75% if questions are used to score

Sample Running Record

Line	Text From *Arthur Writes a Story* by Marc Brown	The Child's Reading	Running Record
	Page 1	**Page 1**	**Page 1**
1	Arthur's teacher, Mr. Ratburn, explained the	Arthur's teacher, Mr. Ratbur ex..plain...explained the	✓✓✓ ①Ratburn/Ratburn ex..explain..✓ explained ✓
2	homework.	homework.	✓
3	"What should the story be about?" Arthur asked.	"What should the story be about?" asked Arthur.	✓✓✓✓✓ ②③ ④(Arthur/asked)
4	"Anything," Mr. Ratburn said. "Write about something	"Anything," Mr. Ratbur said. "Write all about	✓✓ Ratbur/Ratburn ✓✓ all ✓✓
5	that is important to you."	something that is important to you."	✓✓ impor.../important ✓✓
	Page 2	**Page 2**	
1	Arthur started his story the minute he got home.	Arthur started the story the minute he got home.	✓✓ the/his ⑤ ✓✓✓✓✓
2	He knew exactly what he wanted to write about.	[skips line and turns page]	sc sc just/— exactly/— ⑥ sc sc sc sc —/8 —/about ⑦
	Page 3	**Page 3**	
1	"How I Got My Puppy Pal"	"How I Got My Puppy Pal" [starts over] He knew	✓✓✓✓
2	I always wanted a dog, but first I	just what he wanted to write. "How I Got My Puppy Pal"	✓✓✓✓✓ ⑨H...T/prove ⑧
3	had to prove I was responsible. So I	I always wanted a dog, but first I had to...um...um prove I was re...re...I don't know	✓✓ re..re..re../responsible T ⑩ ✓✓
4	started Arthur's Pet Business. My mom	this...responsible. So I started Arthur's Pet bus...e...ness.business My mom	✓✓✓ bus..e..ness..✓/business
5	made me keep all the animals in the	made me keep all the animals in the	✓✓✓✓✓✓
6	basement. It was a lot of work, but	Base...basement. It was a lot of work, but	base...✓/basement ✓✓✓✓✓✓
7	it was fun, until I thought I lost	it was fun, until I thought I lost	✓✓✓✓✓✓

Taking Running Records Scholastic Professional Books

8	Perky. But then I found her, and	✓✓ ⑪ when/then ✓✓✓
9	she had three puppies! And I got	✓✓✓✓ ✓
10	to keep one of them. That's how	✓✓✓ um/them ✓
11	I got my dog Pal.	✓✓✓ ✓
12	The End	✓✓
Page 4	**Page 4**	
1	Arthur read his story to D.W.	✓✓ ✓✓
2	"That's a boring story," D.W. said. "Does it have to be	✓✓ bad/boring ✓✓✓✓✓✓
3	real life? Because your life is so dull."	✓✓✓✓ ✓✓ dull
4	"I don't want to write a boring story," said Arthur.	✓✓✓✓✓ bad/boring ✓✓
5	"If it w...were me," D.W. suggested, "I'd make the story	✓✓ ✓✓ said/suggested I'd ✓✓✓
6	about getting an elephant."	✓✓ done/more ✓✓✓ would ✓✓
Notes		17 miscues 174 words in Passage

174 − 17 = 157 (words read correctly)

157/174 = 90% (accuracy)

<u>Several words were decoded with closer analysis —</u> i.e. explained important, basement. He omitted the second line on p.2 and was directed to go back to it (SO – start over). I think he was just anxious to read Arthur's story. We discussed the meaning of dull. He understood what boring meant, but didn't recognize the word. Most miscues did not interrupt meaning. He understood and enjoyed the story. He talked about caring for his dog and about friends giving you ideas for stories.

Scoring the Oral Reading of *Arthur Writes a Story*—Step by Step

(Adapted from Clay, 1993; Goodman & Burke, 1972; Johns, 1993; Leslie & Caldwell, 1990)

STEPS	COMMENTARY
❄ Tally the number of errors and correct words.	The section of the book read had 174 words. The child made 17 errors or miscues (each is numbered). He read 157 out of 174 words correctly.
❄ Note that trials that are eventually correct do not count as errors.	The reader made repeated tries at words (i.e., *explained, important, business*) before eventually getting them. These are not errors. With closer analysis, the child can figure them out, but they are not sight words.
❄ Note that insertions add errors. A reader could have more errors than there are words in a line. However, the reader cannot have more errors than words on a page. If the error count for a page does exceed the number of words on it, use the latter as a count of errors for that page.	The reader inserted the word *all* (error # 4). It didn't interfere with meaning.
❄ If a word, line, or sentence is omitted, count each word as an error. If a page is omitted because two were turned at once, don't count the missed words as errors. Adjust the total number of possible words when you're calculating the accuracy percent.	The reader missed the second line on page two in his hurry to get to Arthur's story. When he read the title of the story, I realized his omission and asked him to go back, **S**tart **O**ver (**SO** - #6) at line two on page two, and continue reading from there. He read most of the line correctly. This resulted in 3 errors (# 6— the **SO**, # 7—a substitution of *just* for *exactly*, and # 8—the omission of *about*) instead of 9 errors for each omitted word in the line.
❄ Count a repeated substitution for the same word (e.g., *home* for *house, lady* for *woman*) as an error each time. Consistent substitutions of proper names (e.g., *Timmy* for *Tommy*), however, are only counted the first time. If a different name is substituted (changed to *Tammy* for *Tommy*), an additional error is scored.	The reader read *Ratbur* for *Ratburn* (the teacher's name). It only counted as an error the first time (error # 1). He substituted *bad* for *boring* two times (errors #12 and #14) and each time an error was counted.

* There is a one-to-one count of words on the page and utterances by the reader. If the reader reads two words for one (i.e., for a contraction), two errors are scored.

reader:	do	not
text:	don't	^

    Do for don't is scored as a substitution and *not* is scored as an insertion.
    If a reader reads an entire phrase incorrectly, each word misread counts as an error. If it is self-corrected, each word corrected becomes a self-correction.

The reader read *I would* for *I'd,* and I score the substitution and the insertion as errors (error #16 and #17).

---

* When a word is read as two words (i.e., a / way instead of *away*), it is regarded as a pronunciation error and not counted unless what is said is matched to another word (i.e., *away with* is read *a way with*).

---

* If the child is asked to start over, that counts as a single error. The rereading—not the first reading—is scored. It is advisable to have the reader start over when he has significantly lost meaning and accuracy. The additional error is offset by the number of self-corrections that follow the rereading.

I asked the reader to start over at page 2, line 2 and counted the SO as an error (#6). I scored errors #7 and #8 based on his rereading of that line.

---

* Dialectal or characteristic ways of saying words are not scored as errors.

The reader said *um* for *them* (page 3, line 10). This was typical of his speech. He meant *them*.

---

* If the reader begins to invent the text, stop scoring it as a running record, but continue to take notes on the quality of the inventing. Observe how well the invention matches the gist of the text and illustrations on the page, the reader's use of expression, and any attempts of one-to-one word matching. Share your observations with the reader.

Feedback must be positive but truthful. Celebrate what the reader can do. Let him know that you believe growth is continuing. If you stop recording, he'll immediately feel a sense of failure. You might say, *You did a great job continuing the story in your own way. You made the story match the pictures on the page and go in the order the author intended. And you used lots of expression. When we practice more, you'll be able to read the whole book in the author's words.* If possible, find an easier book so that the child can read the actual words.

Relating Reading Accuracy to Reading Levels

I must know the child's current reading levels to be sure that she has an appropriate book for different reading situations. A running record provides this information. Using the percent of accuracy you've calculated for text processing and the reading levels benchmarks (see Levels Attained on the Running Record, Accuracy, Chapter 3, page 47) you can determine whether the chosen text is at this reader's level: independent (can read by himself), instructional (can read with help), or frustrational (can't read right now) (Clay, 1987). You can also factor in comprehension (meaning-processing) by adding retelling benchmarks to the Clay (1987) accuracy levels. Both accuracy and comprehension must be considered in matching the child with a text (see Attained on the Running Record, Comprehension, Chapter 3, page 47).

If word-reading accuracy and comprehension scores do not fall within the same reading-level category, it's up to the teacher to determine a level, and that level should emphasize comprehension efficiency. Thus, if accuracy is 97% but comprehension is only satisfactory (teacher assessment based on the child's general or structured retelling), the overall conclusion would be that the book is at the child's instructional level. The child could have processed words with a high degree of accuracy without efficiently attending to meaning. If the accuracy was 91% and comprehension was fragmented, the overall conclusion would be that the book was at the child's frustrational level. He read words but did not adequately understand the message.

Sometimes comprehension is higher than word-reading accuracy. In this case, a child may be overrelying on background knowledge—omitting unimportant words and using synonyms—but not picking up new details or cross-checking previous assumptions. Such errors may not inhibit comprehension of a particular text, but the lack of attention to the author's words has the potential to cause misinterpretation and become habitual and problematic. I report results according to the benchmarks (page 47) but add a qualifier whenever I feel that calculations alone may misrepresent the child's performance. For example, if the accuracy was 85% and comprehension was satisfactory, I'd identify the text as borderline frustrational. From observations I've noted, I give evidence for my conclusions in a comment area on the reporting sheet.

> With an accuracy of 85% and satisfactory comprehension, the calculations indicate that this text is borderline frustrational level for Tim. He appears to have relied heavily on prior knowledge of the topic and failed to pick up new information presented in the passage. It wasn't totally frustrational since he got the main idea, but he needs support and guided instruction in critical reading skills. Several word substitutions seem to have created confusion with new facts and terminology in the passage. Tim effectively uses background knowledge but needs to read critically to

affirm, correct, or add to his base of information on a topic if he is to expand it. He agreed to listen to the tape, note his miscues, and then try repeated readings to build fluency and improved comprehension. We also talked about pacing reading, especially on informational passages. His assumption that the text will only be a repeat of known facts tends to cause inefficient reading.

Error-Frequency Rate

Running Record Record

_____ Gr. _____ Date ___

_____ Familiar ___

: ____ E freq: **26** Reading rate: ____ fast

_full ____ satisfactory ____ fragmented or

The error-rate score is an approximation of the number of words a child reads correctly before the flow is interrupted with a miscue. The error frequency gives an indication of fluency and correlates with comprehension. Connections within and across sentences are richer when readers take in information in meaningful units. The higher the score, the greater the meaningful intake before the flow of language and thought is interrupted. To obtain the error-frequency rate (E freq.), divide the number of words in the selection by the number of errors.

Example: If the text had a total of 182 words (as in the accuracy example above) and the reader made 7 errors, I'd divide 182 by 7 and get 26 (round to the whole number if necessary). This shows that the reader makes approximately 1 error every 26th word.

Self-Correction Rate

Running Re

der _____ Gr

Read_____

uracy: ____% SC: $\frac{2}{7}$ E freq: ____ Read

prehension: ____ full ____ satisfactory _

The self-correction figure indicates the degree of self-monitoring and self-maintenance that a reader uses. Students who expect reading to make sense will recognize when they make errors. Those who have begun to take charge of their reading will work to fix the problem. They'll self-correct miscues that don't make sense and interrupt meaning. The goal is to increase the number of miscues that are self-corrected.

Uncorrected miscues inhibit efficient comprehension. If you celebrate self-correction, consistently drawing attention to it, children will increase their efforts to do it. When I give feedback on a reading session, I always comment on the self-corrections I observe: *I could tell you were thinking about what you were reading when you corrected this word and again, here, when you went back to reread and fix these errors. Good readers use fix-up strategies like this. You're doing more self-correcting than before.*

To report the self correction-frequency rate (SC freq.), write the number of self-corrections the reader made above the number of uncorrected errors (this is merely a report, not to be calculated). You want to see the number on top increase and become higher than the one on the bottom.

Example: In our example, the reader had 7 uncorrected errors and 2 self-corrections. Remember, the self-corrections don't count as

Therefore, 7 were scored as errors. A higher number above the line (corrected miscues) reflects a reader's self-monitoring.

$$\text{Sc freq.} = \frac{2}{7} \frac{\text{(corrected miscues)}}{\text{(uncorrected miscues)}}$$

I note children's self-correction frequency rates and plan demonstrations of this strategy when I read aloud. I verbalize my thinking to show what I'm doing. I can self-correct miscues immediately or reread to fix one, going back to any that confused meaning: *Uh-oh, wait a minute. That didn't sound right. I must have mixed something up. I better reread this sentence. Oh, there it is. It says ...., not ....! I'll read this part over. (Read the sentence over with the corrected miscue and continue.) Now, it sounds right!*

I also draw attention to good models of self-correcting when children are reading aloud for the class: *Billy, without any help, you corrected two words that you first made miscues on. How did you know they were wrong, and how did you figure them out?*

Billy: It was talking about the kinds of businesses or jobs or like that. I didn't know the word at first. It looked like induct, *so I said that. Then, I thought it had to be like a company and tried it again and I thought of* industries *when I started to say it again with a /s/ in the /dus/ part.*

Sample Records for Oral Reading

The following running records provide examples of how to code them. Running records are coded item by item and include accuracy, error-frequency, and self correction-frequency scores. I'll discuss the structured retellings that accompanied these readings in Chapter 4 and discuss the analysis of the errors in Chapter 6, where records are repeated with error analysis columns filled in. As you study these samples, review the coding system detailed on pages 37–42 of this chapter.

You're a Recorder Now

You've done it! You've closely observed readers in your class and noted every reading strategy they used and every behavior they exhibited. You've gathered objective data and computed word-reading accuracy, self-correction frequency, and error frequency. You're noticing patterns in children's development and tailoring your teaching to these observations to meet each student's specific needs.

The next step is to assess students' comprehension of what they've read. Although you've been informally checking their understanding, now is the time to formalize this part of the process. The next chapter will show you time to formalize this part of the process. The next chapter will show you how to standardize retellings to evaluate specific aspects of the reader's comprehension.

Practice Together! Learn More!

※ With grade-level teachers, a school team, or professional colleagues, practice analyzing running-record markings in the line-by-line samples provided here. Examine the miscues and self-corrections and note repetitions, particularly where they resulted in self-corrections. Also notice that these records include examples of readings that omit pauses for punctuation, which can result in confused meanings. Share your interpretations of each reading sample and discuss what you'd plan for your next teaching step with each child. What specific skills need to be taught or reinforced? Are there strategies that the child uses but confuses?

※ Discuss and share records you've written in your class with colleagues. You'll gather different perspectives and suggestions for teaching. Do you find common errors at your grade level? Are there indications of common needs for strategy instruction? Is there evidence in the records of a need for curricular changes—in the classroom, grade level, or school?

Sample Running Record

Sean, reading *If You Traveled on the Underground Railroad*

Page	Text	Sean's Reading
pg. 47	When was the best time of year to escape?	When was the best time of year to escape?
	Some people said summer, some said winter.	Some people said summer some said winter.
	If you traveled in summer, you didn't have to worry	If you travel in summer you didn't have to wor..
	about the cold. The trees were green, and there were	about the cold—worry about the cold. The trees were green and there was
	lots of berries and small animals for food. But it was	a lot of berries and small animals to find for food. But it was
	also easier for the hunters to follow you.	also easy for the hunters to find you.
	Winter, of course, could be bitter cold. But there	Winter, of c..c.cuz could be cold. But that
	were good reasons for going then. The rivers were	was good reason—reasons—for going then. The rivers were
	often frozen. You could cross them by walking on the	often. You could cross them by walking on the
	ice. In the summer you might have to find a boat.	ice. In the summer you might have to find a boat.
	Many slaves ran away at Christmas. Their owners	Many slaves ran away at Christmas. Their owners
	were so busy going to parties, they might not notice	were busy going to parties, they might not notice
	for several days that a slave was missing. That would	for several days that a slave was missing. That would
	give you a head start.	give you a head start.
	Whether it was summer or winter, certain days	When it was summer or winter cer—days
	were better than others for your escape. Saturday was	were better—some days were better—than others for your escape. Saturday was
	best. The newspapers wouldn't print advertisements	best. The news...newspapers wouldn't write ad-ver..stories
	on Sunday. And so the owners couldn't tell everyone	on Sunday. And so the owners couldn't tell everyone
	that you had run off. That also gave you a head start.	that you had run off. That also gave you a head start.
pg. 48	And whether it was summer or winter, you hoped	And when it was summer or winter, you hoped
	for clear nights. Then you could look up at the sky	for clear nights. Then you could look up at the sky
	and follow the North Star. It pointed toward freedom.	and follow the North Star. It pointed towards freedom.

Pg.		# E	# SC	Error match M	S	L-S
47	✓ ✓ ✓ ✓ ✓ ✓ ✓ ✓					
	✓ ✓ ✓ ✓ ⓪ ✓ ✓ ✓					
	✓ ✓ ~~travel~~ / traveled ✓ ✓ ⓪ ✓ ✓ ✓ ✓ ✓ was/worry ˢᶜ	1	1			
	(✓ ✓ ᴿ ✓ ✓ ✓ ✓ ⓪ ✓ ✓ was/were)	1				
	a lot/ₐ lots ✓ ✓ ✓ ✓ ˢᶜ ᵗᵒ/for find ˢᵉ/food ✓ ✓ ✓	2	2			
	✓ easy/easier ✓ ✓ ✓ find/follow ᴿ ✓	2				
	✓ ✓ c...sn.SU2/course ✓ ✓ (bitter) ✓ ✓ that/there	3				
	was/were ✓ ✓ reason/reasons ˢᶜ ✓ ✓ ✓ ✓ ✓ ✓	1	1			
	✓ (frozen) ✓ ✓ ✓ ✓ ✓ ✓ ✓	1				
	✓ ✓ ✓ ✓ ✓ ✓ ✓ ✓ ✓ ✓					
	✓ ✓ ✓ ✓ ✓ ✓ ✓					
	✓ (so) ✓ ✓ ✓ ✓ ✓ ✓ ✓	1				
	✓ ✓ ✓ ✓ ✓ ✓ ✓ ✓ ✓ ✓					
	✓ ✓ ✓ ✓ ✓					
	when/whether ✓ ✓ ✓ ✓ ✓ ⓪ some/her certain ✓	2				
	(✓ ✓ ᴿ ✓ ✓ ✓ ✓ ✓ ✓ ✓)					
	✓ ✓ news.../newspapers ✓ write/print other/advertisements stories	2				
	✓ ✓ ✓ ✓ ✓ ✓ ✓ ✓					
	✓ ✓ ✓ ✓ ✓ ✓ ✓ ✓ ✓ ✓ ✓					
48	✓ when/whether ✓ ✓ ✓ ✓ ✓ ✓ ✓	1				
	✓ ✓ ✓ ✓ ✓ ✓ ✓ ✓ ✓					
	✓ ✓ ✓ ✓ ✓ ✓ ✓ towards/toward ✓	1				

18   4

$$accuracy = \frac{182}{200} = 91\%$$

$$E\ freq.: = \frac{200}{18} = 11 = \text{an error on every 11th word}$$

$$SC\ freq.: = \frac{4}{18} = \text{4 errors corrected and 18 left uncorrected}$$

Sample Running Record: Lisa, reading *Nana Upstairs & Nana Downstairs*

Page	Text	Lisa's Reading
pg. 1	When Tommy was a little boy, he had a grandmother and a great-grandmother. He loved both of them very much.	When Tommy was a little boy he had a grandmother and a great-grandmother He loved both of them very much.
pg 2	He and his family would go to visit every Sunday afternoon. His grandmother always seemed to be standing by the big black stove in the kitchen.	He and his family would go to visit on Sunday .... His grandma always seemed~~see~~ to be standing~~st stand~~ᴿ by the big black stove in the kitchen.
pg. 3	His great-grandmother was always in bed upstairs because she was ninety-four years old.	His great-grandma was always in bed upstairs~~up stairs~~ because she was ...ninety...fourᴿ years old.
	So Tommy called them Nana Downstairs and Nana Upstairs.	So Tommy called them Nana......Downstairs and Nana Upstairs.
pg. 4	Almost every Sunday was the same. Tommy would run into the house, say hello to his Grandfather Tom, and Nana Downstairs and then go up the back stairway to the bedroom where Nana Upstairs was.	Almost every Sunday was the same Tommy would run into the house and say hello to his Grandpa Tom and Nana .... Downstairs and then go up the back stairs to the bedroom where Nana Upstairs was.
pg. 5	"Get some candy," Nana Upstairs would say. And he would open the lid of the sewing box on the dresser, and there would be candy mints.	"Get some candy," Nana Upstairs would say. And he would open the cover of lid the sewing box .... on the bureau and there would be candies.ᴿ
pg. 6	Once Nana Downstairs came into the bedroom and helped Nana Upstairs to the big Morris chair and tied her in so she wouldn't fall out.	Once Nana Downstairs came into the bedroom and helped Nana Upstairs to the big Man's chair and tried~~tied~~ her in so she wouldn't fall out.
	"Why will Nana Upstairs fall out?" Tommy asked.	"Why will Nana Upstairs fall out?" Tommy asked.
	"Because she is ninety-four years old," Nana Downstairs said.	"Because she is ninety-four years old," Nana Downstairs said.
	"I'm four years old," Tommy said. "Tie me in a chair too!"	"I'm four years old," Tommy said. "Tie me in a chair too!"
pg. 7	So every Sunday, after he found the candy mints in the sewing box on the dresser, Nana Downstairs would come up the back stairway and tie Nana Upstairs and Tommy in their chairs, and then they would eat their candy and talk.	So every Sunday, after he found the candy mints~~candies~~ ..... in the sewing box on the dresser~~dress~~ᴿ Nana Downstairs would come up the back stairs and tie Nana Upstairs and Tommy in their chairs, and then they would eat their candies and talk.

Taking Running Records Scholastic Professional Books

Sample Running Record: Lisa, reading *Nana Upstairs & Nana Downstairs*

Pg.		# E	# SC	Error match M	S	L-S
1	✓✓✓✓✓✓ ② ✓✓					
	✓✓✓✓✓					
	✓✓✓✓✓✓					
2	✓✓✓✓✓✓✓					
	on/Every ✓ H (afternoon) ✓ grandma/grandmother	3				
	✓ se/seemed ✓✓ at.stand. se/standing R ✓✓✓		2			
	✓✓					
3	✓✓ grandma/grandmother ✓✓✓	1				
	✓ up.stairs ✓/upstairs ✓✓✓ H ✓ H ✓ R					
	✓✓					
	✓✓✓✓ H ✓					
	✓✓✓					
4	✓✓✓✓✓✓					
	✓✓✓✓✓ ② and ✓ ∧	1				
	✓✓✓ grandpa/grand.father ✓ ② ✓✓	1				
	H ✓✓✓✓✓✓					
	stairs/stairway ✓✓✓✓	1				
	✓✓					
5	✓ ✓ ✓ ✓ ✓					
	✓✓✓✓✓ ✓ sc cover/lid ✓		1			
	✓ sc (sewing sc box) ✓ R ✓ bureau/dresser ✓✓	1	2			
	✓✓ candies/candy (mints)	2				
6	✓✓✓✓✓					
	✓✓✓✓✓✓					
	✓ Manis/Morris ✓✓ ✓ tried se/tied ✓✓✓	1	1			
	✓✓✓					
	✓✓✓✓✓					
	✓✓					
	✓✓✓✓✓✓					
	✓✓					
	✓✓✓✓✓					
	✓✓✓✓					
7	✓✓✓✓✓✓					
	candies sc A-T/Candy (mints) R ✓✓✓✓✓	1	1			
	grass A-T/dresser ✓✓✓✓✓	1				
	✓✓ stairs/stairway ✓✓✓✓	1				
	✓✓✓✓✓✓					
	✓✓✓ candies/Candy ✓✓	1				
		15	7			

accuracy = $\frac{214}{229}$ = 93%

E freq.: = $\frac{214}{15}$ = 15 = an error every 15th word

SC freq.: = $\frac{7}{15}$ = 7 corrected errors and 15 left uncorrected

* I added the child's reading for illustration purposes only. This is not part of taking a running record.

Sample Running Record
Jamie, reading *Shadows Are About*

Page	Text	Jamie's Reading
pg. 1	It is day. The sun is out.	It is day. The sun is out.
pg. 3	Inside, outside, shadows are about.	Inside ~ In...side, outside ~ out...side shadows are around.
pg. 5	They drive with cars and sway with trees.	They drive with cars and swing with trees
pg. 7	They droop with flowers and fall with leaves.	They drop with flowers and fall with leaves.
pg. 9	They stretch with cats and chase with dogs.	They stand with cats and ch..ch..run with dogs.
pg. 10	They swim with ducks and jump with frogs.	They swim with ducks and jump with frogs.
pg. 12	Shadows run. Shadows skip.	Shadows run. Shadows sk...sk skip ip.
pg. 13	Sometimes shadows turn a flip.	Some....times they Sometimes ..S. to a flip R
pg. 14	They flap with flags...	They fly with flags...
pg. 15	...and swoop with kites.	...and swing with kites.
pg. 16	They roll with hoops...	They roll with hoops...
pg. 17	...and race with bikes.	...and race with bikes.
pg. 18	Shadows hop. Shadows stand.	Shadows hop. Shadows stand.
	Shadows march beside a band.	Shadows m...m... march be-side beside a band.
pg. 20	Late-day shadows stretch through rooms.	Long-day shadows start the rooms
	They sit with chairs and lean with brooms.	They sit with.... chairs and t..ē..an lean with brooms R
pg. 22	Shadows climb up and down.	Shadows climb up and down.
pg. 23	Shadows bounce around.....around.	Shadows jump bounce around... around.
pg. 24	They clap with hands and roll with balls.	They clap with hands and roll with balls.
	They paint dark pictures on the walls.	They pain paint d..ark dark p..pic pictures on the walls.
pg. 26	But when the day turns into night....	But when the day ...turns.... into night...
pg. 28	...shadows never stay...without a light.	...shadows never stay.. with...out without a light.

Taking Running Records Scholastic Professional Books

Sample Running Record

Jamie, reading *Shadows Are About*

Pg.		# E	# SC	Error match M	S	L-S
1	✓✓ ✓ ✓ ✓ ✓					
3	in...side✓ out...side✓ ✓ ✓ around about / Inside outside	1				
5	✓✓✓✓ swing/away ✓✓	1				
7	✓ drop/droop ✓✓✓ ✓ ✓	1				
9	✓ stand/stretch ✓✓✓ ch..ch..run/chase ✓✓	2				
10	✓✓ ✓ ✓ ✓ ✓ ✓					
12	✓ ✓ ✓ sk...sk..ip✓/SKIP					
13	some..times✓/sometimes ✓ (turn)✓✓ᴿ do	1				
14	✓ fly/flap ✓✓	1				
15	✓ swing/swoop ✓✓	1				
16	✓ ✓ ✓ ✓					
17	✓ ✓ ✓ ✓					
18	✓ ✓ ✓ ✓					
20	✓ m..rm...A..I/march be..side✓/beside ✓✓	1				
20	Long/Late ✓ ✓ start the/stretch through ✓	3				
	✓ ✓ ✓ H ✓ ✓ tr..E..dn se/Jean ✓✓ᴿ		1			
22	✓ ✓ ✓ ✓ ✓					
23	✓ jump sc/bounce ✓ ✓		1			
24	✓ ✓ ✓ ✓ ✓ ✓ ✓					
	✓ pa n sc/paint d..ark✓/dark p...pie✓/pictures ✓✓✓		1			
26	✓ ✓ ✓ ✓ (turns)...✓✓ A..T	1				
28	✓ ✓ ✓ with...out✓/without ✓ ✓					

13   3

accuracy = $\frac{116}{129}$ = 89.9 = 90%

E freq.: $\frac{129}{13}$ = 9.9 = 10 = an error every 10th word

SC freq.: $\frac{3}{13}$ = 3 corrected errors and 13 left uncorrected

Running-Record Recording Form

Reader _____ Gr. _____ Date _____ Recorder _____

Text Read_____ Familiar ____ Unfamiliar ____ Genre _____

Accuracy: ____% SC: ____ E freq: ____ Reading rate: ___ fast ___ av. ___ slow Text level: _____

Comprehension: ____ full ____ satisfactory ____ fragmented or % ____ on questions asked

Comments_____

_____

_____

_____

Reading level for this text: ____ independent ____ instructional ____ frustrational

Pg.		# E	# SC	Error match		
				M	**S**	**L-S**
		Totals:				

Adapted from Marie Clay's *An Observational Survey Of Early Literacy Achievement (1993)*.

Pg.		# E	# SC	Error match		
				M	S	LS

Adapted from Marie Clay's *An Observational Survey Of Early Literacy Achievement (1993)*.

Running-Record Recording Form

Here's where you'd write narrative, informational, poetry, etc.

Reader _____ Gr. _____ Date _____ Recorder ____

Text Read_____ Familiar ____ Unfamiliar ____ Genre _____

Accuracy: ____% SC: ____ E freq: ____ Reading rate: ___ fast ___ av. ___ slow Text level: ____

This is the difficulty level, readability level, or grade level of the book.

Comprehension: ____ full ____ satisfactory ____ fragmented or % ____ on questions asked

This is your overall judgment on the quality of the retelling.

If you've used your own questions as a comprehension check, you can calculate a percent score.

Comments_____

Here's where you write general comments on the overall performance.

Reading level for this text: ____ independent ____ instructional ____ frustrational

See pages 47 and 91 to determine this level.

Totals

This is where you record the **Total** number of errors and self-corrections

When you know what book will be used, fill in page numbers before the child reads. Otherwise, fill in as many as you can while taking the record.

Tally errors and self corrections line by line and record numbers.

Pg.		# E	# SC	Error match M	S	L-S

M stands for meaning, **S** for syntax, and **L-S** for letter-sound. If the miscue held meaning intact, put a **Y** (for yes) in the **M** box. If the miscue fit syntactically (grammatically and/or structurally), put a **Y** in the **S** box. If the miscue had similar letters and sound matches, put a **Y** in the **L-S** box. A dash (—) means it did not match in these areas. **Note:** I fill these boxes in later — after taking the running record.

CHAPTER 4

Retellings: Readers Show What They Know

You've practiced recording children's oral reading, marking miscues and the words read correctly in order to assess fluency in word recognition. This is the first part of a complete running record. Although smooth reading of words is essential for efficient comprehension, it doesn't guarantee it. It's possible for a child to say the words with a high degree of accuracy without processing any meaning. I've worked with children who did this. Therefore the child's understanding of what he reads needs to be assessed apart from the assessment of his accuracy with the words. Without meaning, the activity is not reading—it's word calling.

The process for systematically assessing children's understanding of what they've read is called *retelling*. The teacher asks the child to retell what she has just read. Although I'll focus on using retelling to complete full running records, retellings may also be used after silent reading (D.E.A.R. time) or during a guided-reading session. You might also ask the child to retell the content of a teacher read-aloud to assess listening comprehension. Whenever they're used, retellings are a highly effective strategy for assessing a reader's overall comprehension of a text.

Mrs. Hiwiller takes a running record with Tim.

Why Use Retelling?

Retellings are a valuable assessment tool because with them, readers:

- ❊ demonstrate what they remember about the main ideas and the details of the text.

- ❊ integrate personal interpretations and connections.

- ❊ learn to self-monitor their comprehension in a structured way as they internalize the process.

- ❊ come to understand that reading requires critical thinking, understanding, and the construction of meaning with text. They realize that merely saying words is not enough.

- ❊ anticipate having to retell and consequently become more engaged with the text, more sensitive to the possibility of varied interpretations, and more aware of text structures.

- ❊ become *active* readers projecting themselves into a text—to view story events, relationships, and facts as a participant rather than an observer.

- ❊ develop expressive oral-language skills, building fluency and confidence in oral presentations of personal ideas.

- ❊ develop more sophisticated language structures for relating their own stories and anecdotes.

TEACHING TIP

Add a New Twist

Ideally the reader will retell the text to someone who hasn't ever read it, as would happen in everyday, literacy-related interactions. However, in the classroom setting, retelling to someone who knows the content is often necessary. So, to add a dimension of surprise and interest for the listener and stimulate creativity in the teller, you might have the child retell the content in a new way, such as retelling from a character's point of view.

Making Retellings Meaningful

If you have a consistent way of monitoring your students' retellings, you'll be able to use your notes, along with the running-records text scores, to plan effective instruction. You can standardize retellings by using checklists to assess the performance as children retell what they've read. Have them follow an appropriate graphic organizer as a guide when they retell (see pages 71–72 for examples).

Preparing the Students

Explain to children that the order, content, and sequence of the retelling is based on the kind of writing (genre) that was read. Using the graphic organizers provided on pages 70–72, review the concept of story grammar—characters, setting, problem, events, and resolution—as a guide for retelling narratives. Also review informational-text structures (frames)—comparison, proposition with support, cause and effect, description, collections, and sequence—as guides for retelling in that genre.

Be sure you've introduced, modeled, and had the children practice with each graphic organizer and checklist before you use it for retelling. The children need to know exactly what you expect of them. Review and post the "Telling Someone All About What You Read" list as a reminder. Model retelling across several different types of texts.

Graphic organizers that match text structures trigger recall and stimulate students to interpret what they read. After children become familiar

Guidelines for Telling Someone All About What You Read

1 **Decide what kind of selection (genre or kind of writing) you read.**
Identify the genre for the text you read. Then begin with an introduction: Name of the text read) by _____ is all about _____.

2 **If it is a story or narrative, use one of those organizers to guide you.**
The choice depends on whether you read part of a story or the whole thing.
As you talk and retell, follow the organizer and tell about each topic. If you read only part of a story, follow that organizer and pass over anything on the list that does not apply to what you read. For example, if character traits are not clearly revealed in the section you read, you won't have a lot to say about that.

3 **If it's an informational or expository text, decide what the main structure in the section is.**
Use that organizer as you retell what you've read. For example, if the section was talking about causes and effects for a volcano's eruption, you'd start by explaining that volcanoes erupt. Then, you'd tell what you've learned about the causes for eruptions. Finally, you'd explain the effects of eruptions as they were described by the author. You may follow more than one of the organizers if the section you read has more than one structure. For example, there may have been description before a problem was identified and a solution offered by the author.

4 **Don't forget to add your own ideas, interpretations, and connections to experiences or other books when retelling.**
Tell how you feel about the story or information. For example, tell what was exciting or interesting.
Tell how this story or information is like or different from what you knew before.
Tell if you think the author wrote in a way that is interesting and easy to understand.
Tell if you think the story is realistic or the information is accurate.

with graphic organizers and use them in independent and guided work, they see them as valuable tools for reading and retelling. During reading, they serve as a mental framework for processing content. During a retell, they act as or become a visual guide for remembering and organizing content. Post graphic organizers around the room to make them readily available for students to refer to.

When you model retelling, be sure to demonstrate the thinking that goes with matching a graphic organizer format to the content of the text. Refer to the appropriate graphic organizers for the following examples:

Organizer for Narrative Stories

Name _____ Date _____

Story _____

Characters: (Who)

Setting: (Where and When)

Problem:

Events: (Beginning, Middle, and End)

Solution: (Resolution of the Problem)

Reactions/Comments:

72   *Taking Running Records* Scholastic Professional Books

❋ If it's a story, did I tell all the story parts? *Somebody* (character), *Where* (setting-place), *When* (setting time), *Wanted* (problem), *But* (order of events), *So* (solution). Did I tell what I think, how it's like another book, or what happened to me? (See "Narrative—Complete Story," page 85.)

❋ If it's only a part of a story, did I tell how it connects to what already happened? Tell everything about this part? Tell my ideas about what happened or the writing in this part? Tell what I think will happen next? Tell how it's like another book or what happened to me? (See "Narrative— Section of Text," page 85.)

❋ If it's about comparing, did I tell how they are alike and how they are different? (See "Organizers for Informational Texts—Comparison," page 71.)

❋ If it's a collection, did I name all of them? (See "Organizers for Informational Texts—Collection," page 70)

❋ If it must be a certain way, did I tell the steps in order? (See "Organizers for Informational Texts—Sequence," page 70.)

❋ If the author gave an opinion, did I say what it was and tell his reasons? (See "Organizers for Informational Texts—Theory/Proof," page 71.)

❋ If it described something, did I tell what it was and important details about it? (See "Organizers for Informational Texts—Descriptive," page 70.)

- If it tells a cause for something, did I explain that and what happened because of it (effects)? (See "Organizers for Informational Texts—Causation," page 71.)
- Did I tell what I think?

Post the "Retellings Practice Guide" (page 73) as a wall chart for the children to refer to.

Introduce and explain the scoring checklists (see the narrative and informational checklists on pages 81–83) that correlate with the graphic organizers. First, I have children observe me retelling and collaboratively analyze my efforts to be sure I've covered the essential points on the graphic organizer list. Then, they practice with their peers. Using graphic organizers as a guide for retelling and the points on the checklists to evaluate each other's performance, children notice what needs to be included for a successful retell. This may take a few weeks, but it's well worth the time. After practicing with peers, children meet with me to read one on one and retell.

Getting Started With Retelling Checklists

While learning the marking system for oral reading, you focused on detailed recordings for each word and wrote general observations about the child's retelling. Until you're comfortable with the retelling checklists, do the reverse. Write general observations on the oral reading and practice using the appropriate checklist as the child retells. The next chapter focuses on putting both parts—recording of oral reading and a standardized retelling—together. For now, build comfort with the procedures for retelling and completing a detailed retelling checklist.

Before the reading begins, always make children aware that they will be expected to retell the content of what was read. *This part is about moving waves. When you finish reading, I'll ask you to tell me all about it as if I was someone who never heard it before.*

As you've done before, explain to the children what you'll be doing. The ground rules for retelling won't be a surprise. The children have been thoroughly taught and are comfortable with the task and expectations. You can be confident that their performances will validly reflect their current abilities.

Organizers for Informational Texts

STRUCTURE	CHARACTERISTICS	ORGANIZER
Descriptive	Presents information on a particular topic or gives characteristics of it.	Main Idea and Detail

Main Idea and Detail

M.I.   Details

Semantic Map/Web

subtopic   topic   detail

| **Collection** | Presents a number of ideas or descriptions. How they relate is the focus. The order is unimportant. | List Organizer |

List Organizer

1._____
2._____
3._____
4._____
5._____

| **Sequence** | Presents a number of ideas or descriptions in a prescribed sequence. The order of items is key. | List Organizer or Time Line |

List Organizer or Time Line

1._____
2._____
3._____
4._____
5._____

70

Organizers for Informational Texts (page 2)

STRUCTURE	CHARACTERISTICS	ORGANIZER
Causation	Presents ideas in a causal relationship.	Situation/Cause and Effect Organizer
Comparison	Presents similarities and differences between 2 or more items/ideas.	Venn Diagram
Theory/Proof	Presents a problem or theory with the author's solution or evidence.	T Proof Organizer

effects or results

causes or reasons

situation

1st idea only   2nd idea only

both

opinion   proof

Organizer for Narrative Stories

Name _____ Date _____

Story _____

....

Characters: (Who)

....

Setting: (Where and When)

....

Problem:

....

Events: (Beginning, Middle, and End)

....

Solution: (Resolution of the Problem)

....

Reactions/Comments:

....

 Taking Running Records Scholastic Professional Books

Retellings Practice Guide

Retelling Checklist for a Story

Did I...

	yes	no
...begin with an introduction? "(Name of story) is a story about...."	____	____

Setting:

...tell where the story takes place?	____	____
...tell when the story takes place?	____	____

Characters:

...tell about the main characters?	____	____
...tell about other characters?	____	____

Problem:

...tell about the most important problem?	____	____

Events:

...tell about important events in the story?	____	____
...tell the events in order?	____	____

Resolution:

...tell how the problem was solved?	____	____

Connections:

...tell how this story is like something that happened to me or someone I know, or like another story I read?	____	____

My Ideas:

...tell about predictions I made or ideas I had about the character, problem, or solution?	____	____

Evaluation:

...tell why I liked or didn't like the story?	____	____
...tell what I liked or didn't like about the way the story was written?	____	____

Guiding and Recording the Retelling

Listen to the child's oral reading. Remember that you're only writing general observations—not coded details about each word—on the reading at this time. This will give you a chance to focus on the retelling without missing insights from the oral-reading segment.

When the child has completed the reading, ask her to think about what she's just read for a few minutes and, when ready, tell you all about it as if you were someone who had never heard it before. Listen carefully, without comments or questions, as the child retells all that she remembers about the content and shares personal comments, reactions, and interpretations.

TEACHING TIP

Retelling Checklists are Flexible

You don't have to fill in every blank. Sometimes they are not applicable. For example, if the selection read is from a longer passage, say the first chapter of a book, the problem may not be identified. In this case write **NA** (doesn't apply) in the *problem* space rather than scoring it against the reteller.

You can have a child retell a selection that she just read silently during a guided-reading lesson, using a retelling checklist to assess her comprehension with silent reading.

Retelling Checklist—Informational Text

Name _Sean_   Date _____   Selection _If You Traveled on the Underground Railroad_

THE STUDENT...	UNASSISTED RETELLING	ASSISTED RETELLING
1 Restates main idea	It's about when is it the best time to escape?	
2 Restates subtopic	It talks about why winter and summer are good.	
3 Identifies key terms/ vocabulary		
4 Identifies key people	the slaves	hunters, the slave hunters, owners of slaves
5 Makes inferences	summer is the best time, I think.	The owners wouldn't like to chase them in the winter. It's nasty weather for them too.
6 Recognizes cause & effect		If snow covers the trail, you can get lost.
7 Comprehends sequence of events/details/order of operation	It told why summer's a good time, then why winter is. Then it told about when it would be in the news - paper.	
8 Understands relative importance of subject matter	You'd have to figure this out carefully if you were a slave. you could die or get caught.	
9 Refers to and interprets visuals	NA	
10 Draws conclusions using prior knowledge and information from text		They were brave and wanted freedom real bad. I would too, but I'd be afraid of the hunters.

Level of Comprehension: _____ Full and detailed _✓_ Partial _____ Fragmentary

Comments _Understood overall message - vague and/or confused on details_

Retelling Checklist—Narrative

Name _Jamie_   Date _____

Text _Shadows Are About_

Familiar/Unfamiliar _somewhat_   Background Information (full/limited) _personal experiences_

	Unassisted Retelling	Assisted Retelling	Illustrations Shown
Named main characters.	boy and girl		
Named other characters.		dog and cat	
Named setting (time/place).	at their house	outside, in the car, riding a bike	
Stated initiating event.	wake up and see shadows		
Identified problem.	kids are telling about all the kinds of shadows		
Described attempts to solve the problem.	they find all the shadows and make some		
Identified reaction of main character to attempts and solution of problem.	NA		
Retold story in correct sequence.			needed to look back, but sequence not critical
Made inferences related to the text.	It's a brother and sister. They're reading in bed		
Made connections with other texts or experience.	I raised my shadow on my bike.	My dad can make shadow animals.	
Made evaluative statements about the writing, illustrations or story.			I like the pictures best 'cause I knew about shadows, but the pictures make the kids friendly. I liked the rabbit in the pictures.

Level of Comprehension: _____ Full and detailed _✓_ Partial/Satisfactory _____ Fragmented

Comments _Knows a lot about shadows - relying on prior knowledge._

If a long pause (3–5 seconds) occurs, ask, *Anything else?* to let the child know that she can share more. Record everything she shares under these circumstances in the "Unassisted Retelling" column of the narrative or informational retelling checklist (see pages 81–83 for blank checklists you can copy). This information was shared without help or substantive prompts. Continue to ask for more until the teller indicates that she's finished. At this point, use the checklist as a guide to begin probing for specific information that the child neglected or covered insufficiently. In the "Assisted Retelling" column, note how the child responds to your verbal prompts. Sometimes readers need to reread or examine illustrations to trigger recall. If prompts are not enough and the reader must revisit the text, make note of specific areas where this was necessary.

Have general questions in mind when you probe for further information. Carefully word these so that they don't, in themselves, provide new information to the teller (Goodman & Burke, 1972). Keeping the questions general—not mentioning specifics—will encourage the reader to develop his own insights and interpretations. You can teach children to use these kinds of general questions that focus on specifics when they practice with each other. Post sample questions for children to refer to. Eventually the

Questions to Ask About Stories

Characters: Who is the main character? Other characters?
Who else was in the story? Tell me about them. What was _____ like?
(Use only names mentioned by the teller.)

Setting: Where/when did the story take place?

Plot: Can you think of anything else that happened?
Why did _____ happen? (Use only those events mentioned by the teller.)
What was the problem to be solved?

Theme: What do you think the story was telling you?
Why do you think the author wanted to write the story?
Do you know any other stories that try to tell you the same thing?

Goodman & Burke, 1972

Questions to Ask About Informational Text

Cause/Effect: Why did _____ happen? What happened after _____?

Proposition/Support: What did _____ suggest? Why did _____ think _____?

Description: What did _____ tell us about _____?

Compare/Contrast: How are _____ and _____ alike? How are _____ and _____ different?

teller will be asking himself these questions as a personal check of his comprehension and retelling.

Another Checklist

You can also use the "Comprehensive Rubric for Story Retelling" (see page 84 for a blank form for you to copy) to evaluate your students' understanding of what they read. It addresses five elements of comprehension: story grammar, details, inferences, prediction, and conclusions; makes connections to the reader's life and other texts; and identifies the type of fictional selection. Each category is scored separately on a scale of 1 to 4, with 4 being the highest. The criteria for each level are described as you move across its row. Evaluate and score the reader's retelling against the criteria, category by category. Add clarifications and check off appropriate boxes in the "Story Grammar" section. For example, on Lisa's retelling of *Nana Upstairs and Nana Downstairs*, Story Grammar elements were all checked (except for the one that did not apply) in score box # 4, giving her a score of **4** for that category. She needed prompting to retell Details. Comments were written in score box # 2 for details, giving her a score of **2** for that category. Lisa needed to be prompted for Inferences, Predictions, Conclusions, and Identification of Type for this Fictional Selection, so she received scores of **2** and **3** in those areas. Overall, the text is considered to be at Lisa's instructional level (average between 2 and 3). She can read it with understanding if prompted in some areas of comprehension.

Comprehensive Rubric for Story Retellings

Name: **Lisa**   Date: _____

Story: **Nana Upstairs and Nana Downstairs**   Rdg. Level: ____ Ind. ✓ Instr. ____ Frus.

Comprehension Elements	Score of 1	Score of 2	Score of 3	Score of 4
Story Grammar [4]	Even with prompting, reader is unable to state or confuses elements of story grammar.	With prompting, the reader includes most of the elements of story grammar ([]characters, []setting, []problem, []event sequence, []resolution)	Without prompting, reader includes most of the elements of story grammar ([]characters, []setting, []problem, []event sequence, []resolution)	Without prompting, reader includes all elements of story grammar ([✓]characters, [✓]setting, [✓]problem, [✓]event sequence, []resolution) *NA*
Details [2]	Even with prompting, reader does not include or gives inaccurate details.	With prompting, reader includes some accurate details. *sketchy retelling — questioning brought out recall of details*	Without prompting, reader laces retelling with some significant & accurate details.	Without prompting, reader laces retelling with all significant & accurate details and some minor ones in a subordinate way.
Inferences, Predictions & Conclusions [2]	Even with prompting, reader does not convey understanding of or confuses story inferences, predictions, and/or conclusions.	With prompting, reader conveys understanding of story inferences, predictions, and/or conclusions. *inferences needed to be guided*	Without prompting, reader explains inferences, predictions, and/or conclusions drawn, however they are weak or minimal.	Without prompting, reader explains critical inferences, predictions, and/or conclusions drawn.
Connections to Reader's Life & Other Texts [3]	Even with prompting, reader is unable to make or confuses connections with other texts and/or life experiences.	With prompting, reader makes connections with other texts and/or life experiences.	Without prompting, reader explains connections with other texts and/or life experiences that vaguely relate to this text. *her one grandma is old and sick too*	Without prompting, reader explains connections with other texts and/or life experiences that closely relate to this text.
Type of Fictional Selection (specific genre) [3]	Even with prompting, reader is unable to identify type of fictional selection (i.e., fairy tale, fantasy, mystery, historical fiction, etc.).	With excessive prompting, reader identifies type of fictional selection (i.e., fairy tale, fantasy, mystery, historical fiction, etc.).	With limited prompting, reader identifies type of fictional selection s/he read (i.e., fairy tale, fantasy, mystery, historical fiction, etc.). *story is about his grandma when he was little (personal narrative)*	With limited prompting, reader identifies type of fictional selection s/he read (i.e., fairy tale, fantasy, mystery, historical fiction, etc.).

Comments: *Lisa enjoyed the book. She made connections to visiting her grandma who is very ill. She said her grandma is sweet, like Tomie's.*

Giving Feedback

Following the retelling, share the results of both the reading and retelling with the student. Continually emphasize the importance of both efficient word recognition *and* full comprehension. Share your anecdotal notes on the reading and the checklist observations on the retelling. Here's how a typical conference might go:

Teacher: You read a lot of words correctly. Right here you said, *The children ran to the slide in the playground. They like to slide so high that they seem to touch the sky.* I'll bet you were thinking what you'd run to. But then, you stopped and went back to reread it and read, *The children ran to the swings in the playground. They like to swing so high that they seem to touch the sky.* That was a good self-correction. It shows you were thinking about what you read. How did you know you needed to fix-up that part?

Child: When I heard myself say, *They like to slide so high that they seem to touch the sky*, I knew it wasn't right because you don't slide so high—you slide down after you climb the stairs to the slide. I looked at the word again, and it had *i-n-g*, and I knew it was swing because of that and because you can *swing* up high.

T: You also talked about how they were feeling that day when the new playground was finished. I agree with you. They were proud of it because they helped build it. They'll want to keep it nice. You described the characters, the setting—where and when—the problem the kids had with the bully, and the way they solved it.

C: They weren't afraid. They didn't do bad things back, but they made him feel silly for treating people that way.

T: When you reread this, you could tell me how they made the plan to teach the bully a lesson. Next time, I want you to think about the order of things that happen in the story. Try to think of all the important events that happened to solve the problem.

Celebrating the child's fix-up strategies ensures that he will value and continue them. Make one or two teaching points about errors for each reading. Don't overkill! There'll be opportunities to discuss other points after other readings or in a group mini-lesson. Patterns emerge and provide a basis for selecting miscues to talk about in the debriefing sessions. Such patterns also suggest topics for lessons that are more likely to capture the teachable moment, presenting skills when children are ready to understand them:

Teacher: You retold a lot of details about the characters and setting in this story. I thought you had ideas about why they needed to find the ice-cream seller. When I asked you, you told me you knew she was probably a witness. That's good mystery thinking! Share your own thoughts and opinions in the retelling. Good readers are always thinking ahead and predicting, and I like to hear what clues struck you. You don't have to wait for questions.

Child: She was around the whole time, so I think she has to know something even though she's not telling.

T: We'll see if you're right. Here you read, *Billy found the girl who was selling ice cream.* You misread this word *girl.* Your word made sense, and it sounded right in that part of the sentence. It went along with the picture too, but does the author's word have the letters you'd expect to find in the word *girl*?

C: No, but I don't know that word. The picture looks more like a grown-up; not really a kid, a girl. It's not *woman* either. You'd need a *W*.

T: Putting in a word that means about same as the word you're unsure of is a good strategy that helps you keep going and understand what you've read. Now, we can look back and talk about the word and learn a new word. The author's word starts with *l* and it has a pattern like *shady* with the sounds of the *a* and *y*—*a* sounds like /ā/ and the *y* sounds like /ē/. A *y* at the end of longer words sounds like /ē/. It's /lā/ —/dē/, *lady.* Have you heard the word *lady* used by anyone before?

C: Ya. My mom said a lady came to the door to collect for the food drive. She was a woman.

T: A lady is a grown-up girl or female person. Someone might use the word *woman* when talking about a lady. Your word didn't seem to keep you from understanding what you read, but changing the author's words can make an important difference sometimes. In this mystery, knowing the ice-cream seller is a grown-up lady and not a child might be important.

T: In the next part, you'll find out if the lady can help. When you retell again, I want you to include your own thinking—on your own, so I don't have to ask you questions about your ideas.

End a debriefing with positive, genuine feedback:

Thank you for reading with me. You really showed how you're thinking as you read and using fix-up strategies when things don't make sense. You retold a lot about the story—in the order it happened. Your ideas about why Billy's friends were annoyed with him were interesting. You made that connection to something that happened to you.

What will you be working on now, when you get back to your group? Will you ask Karen to see me? I think I can listen to another reader today.

Your stance as a teacher is that of a neutral, interested observer—just as you would be if you were listening to a child who runs up and excitedly tells you about something he's just read (a natural setting). The objective is to establish a situation in which the teller can comfortably share a full and accurate reading performance that reflects his current level of competence.

Completing the Retelling Checklists

Share your final notes with the reader and use them to set goals for his next retelling. These goals may include: retell more on your own, try to add more details, tell what you think about the author's ideas. A review of the teacher's written comments and boxes filled in clearly show the child which areas he needs to practice and, generally, whether the book was too easy, too hard, or just right. I can easily identify specific comprehension skills that readers are struggling with or attempting to use as I review checklists. Common needs become evident and establish a purpose for small-group strategy lessons. Perhaps some children aren't integrating or making connections with prior knowledge. Others may not be assimilating new vocabulary or key terms that the author has defined for them.

Checks alone etch a skeletal picture of the retelling. The analysis and description of the reader's performance will be richer when the checklist is replete with details. If you taped the sessions, you can review them to augment and clarify information you recorded during the retelling. When you've filled in the forms and looked them over for revisions or additions, evaluate the overall performance on the retelling. Ask yourself, and answer the following questions to assess whether the text is at the appropriate level for this child. Use this thinking to make comments on the checklists.

Q: Was the retelling full and detailed (independent level)?

A: Most of the retelling was unassisted, correct, and included comments that reflected personal connections. Therefore, it appears to be at his independent level.

Q: Was it partial, but satisfactory (instructional level)?

A: About half or several parts of the retell needed to be prompted. Several accurate details were added, however, when questioning was done. The child needed to be guided in comprehending this selection. It is at his instructional level.

Q: Or was it fragmented (frustrational level)?

A: He had a difficult time retelling what was read. Much was left out or confused. Important points were missed. It appears that this selection was too hard or at his frustrational level.

Timetable for Getting Up to Speed With Retelling

You can use the same general schedule that you used for practicing the oral-reading marking system. Meet with one or two children a day while the other children are engaging in independent activities. You'll be able to complete a standardized retelling with each child in two to four weeks. These scheduled standardized retellings follow two to three weeks spent introducing the process, modeling procedures, and allowing practice with peers.

You've now learned and practiced the two parts of a complete running record: using the marking system to record a child's oral reading of a selection and listening to her retelling while writing observations on a checklist to complete a standardized retelling.

The next chapter will focus on doing both parts in one session to create a full running-record.

Practice Together! Learn More!

❋ With a group of colleagues at your grade level, in your school, or at a workshop, analyze the retelling checklists for Sean, Lisa, and Jamie. What insights on each child's comprehension do you have? What strategies do you suppose the child is using? What needs would guide your teaching points and future lessons?

❋ Collect retelling samples from your students. Analyze several of these with colleagues. Can you identify common needs that suggest a focus for schoolwide, staff-development initiatives? Does the staff need to know more about fostering higher-level thinking skills to increase children's ability with comprehension?

Retelling Checklist—Informational Text

Name _____ Date_____ Selection _____

THE STUDENT...	UNASSISTED RETELLING	ASSISTED RETELLING
1 Restates main idea		
2 Restates subtopic		
3 Identifies key terms/ vocabulary		
4 Identifies key people		
5 Makes inferences		
6 Recognizes cause & effect		
7 Comprehends sequence of events/details/order of operation		
8 Understands relative importance of subject matter		
9 Refers to and interprets visuals		
10 Draws conclusions using prior knowledge and information from text		

Level of Comprehension: _____Full and detailed _____Partial _____Fragmentary

Comments_____

10 Questions to Assess Retelling—Informational Text

Name _____ Date _____ Selection _____

	OBJECTIVES	ASSISTED	UNASSISTED	COMMENTS
1	Did the student identify the topic?			
2	Can the student summarize the main idea?			
3	Did the student use any new vocabulary in the retelling?			
4	Was the student able to read and interpret charts, tables, diagrams, and pictures?			
5	Did the students share any extra information that wasn't in the text, in charts, diagrams, etc.?			
6	Did the student indicate that he knew anything about the text before reading it (background knowledge)?			
7	Did the student make a connection between the material and real life (application)?			
8	Can the student connect the material to other subject areas?			
9	Did the student sequence steps that needed to be sequenced (i.e., stages of frogs)?			
10	Is the student willing/able to respond to questions and participate in text activities?			

Level of Comprehension: _____ Full and detailed _____ Partial _____ Fragmentary

Comments _____

Taking Running Records Scholastic Professional Books

Retelling Checklist—Narrative

Name _____ Date _____

Text _____

Familiar/Unfamiliar _____ Background Information (full/limited)_____

	Unassisted Retelling	Assisted Retelling	Illustrations Shown
Named main characters.			
Named other characters.			
Named setting (time/place).			
Stated initiating event.			
Identified problem.			
Described attempts to solve the problem.			
Identified reaction of main character to attempts and solution of problem.			
Retold story in correct sequence.			
Made inferences related to the text.			
Made connections with other texts or experience.			
Made evaluative statements about the writing, illustrations, or story.			

Level of Comprehension: _____ Full and detailed _____ Partial/Satisfactory _____ Fragmented

Comments_____

_____

Comprehensive Rubric for Story Retellings

Name _____ Date _____

Story _____ Rdg. Level: _____ Ind. _____ Instr. _____ Frus.

Comprehension Elements	Score of 1	Score of 2	Score of 3	Score of 4
Story Grammar ☐	Even with prompting, reader is unable to state or confuses elements of story grammar.	With prompting, the reader includes most of the elements of story grammar ([]characters, []setting, []problem, []event sequence, []resolution).	Without prompting, reader includes most of the elements of story grammar ([]characters, []setting, []problem, []event sequence, []resolution).	Without prompting, reader includes all elements of story grammar ([]characters, []setting, []problem, []event sequence, []resolution).
Details ☐	Even with prompting, reader does not include accurate details or gives inaccurate details.	With prompting, reader includes some accurate details.	Without prompting, reader laces retelling with some significant & accurate details.	Without prompting, reader laces retelling with all significant & accurate details and some minor ones in a subordinate way.
Inferences, Predictions, & Conclusions ☐	Even with prompting, reader does not convey understanding of or confuses story inferences, predictions, and/or conclusions.	With prompting, reader conveys understanding of story inferences, predictions, and/or conclusions.	Without prompting, reader explains inferences, predictions, and/or conclusions drawn; however, they are weak or minimal.	Without prompting, reader explains critical inferences, predictions, and/or conclusions drawn.
Connections to Reader's Life & Other Texts ☐	Even with prompting, reader is unable to make or confuses connections with other texts and/or life experiences.	With prompting, reader makes connections with other texts and/or life experiences.	Without prompting, reader explains connections with other texts and/or life experiences that vaguely relate to this text.	Without prompting, reader explains connections with other texts and/or life experiences that closely relate to this text.
Type of Fictional Selection (specific genre) ☐	Even with prompting, reader is unable to identify type of fictional selection (i.e., fairy tale, fantasy, mystery, historical fiction).	With excessive prompting, reader identifies type of fictional selection (i.e., fairy tale, fantasy, mystery, historical fiction.).	With limited prompting, reader identifies type of fictional selection he read (i.e., fairy tale, fantasy, mystery, historical fiction).	With limited prompting, reader identifies type of fictional selection he read (i.e., fairy tale, fantasy, mystery, historical fiction).

Comments_____

_____

M. Shea & A. Cole, 1997.

Outlines for Narrative Readings

Name _____ Date_____

NARRATIVE—COMPLETE STORY	NARRATIVE—SECTION OF TEXT
Identify genre: _____ _____	Identify genre: _____ _____
Somebody (Character(s)): _____ _____	Story grammar revealed thus far: _____ _____
Where (Setting—place): _____ _____	Relationship of event to whole: _____ _____
When (Setting—time): _____ _____	Description of event: _____ _____
Wanted (Problem): _____ _____	Analysis of event: _____ _____

But (Order of Events):
  1. _____
  2. _____
  3. _____
	Character traits revealed: _____ _____

So (Solution): _____ _____	Predictions for next part: _____ _____
Reactions: _____ _____	Connections made: _____ _____
Connections made: _____ _____	

Informational Books As Examples of Various Text Structures

Description
Amosky, J. (1995). *All About Owls*. NY: Scholastic.

De Bourgoing, P. (1995). *Under the Ground*. NY: Scholastic.

Simon, S. (1989). *Storms*. NY: Scholastic.

McMillan, B. (1992). *The Baby Zoo*. NY: Scholastic.

Sequence
Aliki (1992). *Milk From Cow to Carton*. NY: HarperCollins.

Robbins, K. (1991). *Make Me a Peanut Butter Sandwich*. NY: Scholastic.

Brill, M. (1996). *Building the Capitol City*. Danbury, CT: Children's Press

Cause and Effect
Freedman, R. (1980). *Immigrant Kids*. NY: Scholastic.

Farndon, J. (1996). *What Happens When…?* NY: Scholastic.

Wick, W. (1997). *A Drop of Water*. NY: Scholastic.

Lauber, P. (1996). *Hurricanes*. NY: Scholastic.

Fradin, D. (1991). *Explorers*. Danbury, CT: Children's Press

Comparison
Singer, M. (1995). *A Wasp Is Not a Bee*. NY: Scholastic.

Kalman, B. & Everts, T. (1994). *Frogs and Toads*. NY: Crabtree Publishing

Spier, P. (1987). *We the People*. NY: Doubleday.

Problem and Solution
Sullivan, G. (1994). *The Day the Women Got the Vote*. NY: Scholastic.

Masoff, J. (199). *Emergency*. NY: Scholastic.

Bang, M. (1997). *Common Ground*. NY: Scholastic.

Combination
Haskings, J. (1995). *The Day Fort Sumter Was Fired On*. NY: Scholastic.

Aliki (1981). *Digging Up Dinosaurs*. NY: HarperCollins.

Levine, E. (1988). *If You Traveled the Underground Railroad*. NY: Scholastic.

CHAPTER 5

Putting It All Together

So far, you've learned how to take running records to assess children's accuracy in reading words and how to use retelling checklists to assess how well children understand what they read. You've practiced these skills, introduced and modeled the procedures with the children, and allowed plenty of time for the children to practice with you and their peers. Step by step, you've developed and fine tuned special skills for assessing children's word recognition, reading fluency, and reading comprehension. You can identify the specific strengths and needs of readers in your class-room. In the process, you've been building a positive climate for learning and assessing literacy achievement.

Now it's time to put the two pieces of a complete running record togeth-er. I've found that detailed recordings of oral reading and standardized retellings provide a wealth of information on reading behaviors. Combined, they create a standardized, consistent process for assessing children's read-ing levels with various types of texts at different degrees of difficulty. Once I had systematic recordings to support my evaluations, I felt confident when reporting children's reading progress. My running records became the catalyst for daily lessons that met readers' immediate needs. They also provided each child's next teacher with a thorough picture of her literacy development.

Coding and Checklisting During the Same Session

Allow yourself plenty of time at first. After you've had practice, you'll be able to complete a full running record, based on approximately 100 words, in 15–25 minutes. But the first time you do both parts with each child, it may take 10–15 minutes longer.

At this point, the children are fully aware of each step—previewing the selection (determining prior knowledge on the topic), oral-reading procedures (their role and yours), and the retelling process (how to demonstrate their understanding and interpretations of the text). Start out by preparing a comfortable place with text and materials ready. With younger children (late kindergarten or early first grade), you'll want to be ready to work with more than one text since selections are very short and children will complete them quickly. Beyond pre-primer level, one selection will work fine.

GUIDELINES FOR TAKING A COMPLETE RUNNING RECORD
Step by Step

✤ **Remind the child of the purpose of this activity.** Let him know that you want to observe how he reads and makes sense of what he reads. Tell him that comprehension is essential. You want to see how he uses strategies to figure out words he doesn't know, thinks along while reading to understand if something doesn't make sense, and uses good fix-up strategies to correct errors that interrupt comprehension. Briefly review efficient decoding strategies (i.e., clunk steps).

✤ **Start with a brief introduction of the book or section the child will read.** If the book is unfamiliar to the reader, talk about the title, cover, author (particularly if it's one the reader knows), and illustrations. This will help the reader make predictions about its content. If the text is one that the child has read before or is in the process of reading (i.e., a chapter book), have him recall the central theme or summarize what he has already read.

✤ **Remind the child that you'll be asking for a retell when the reading is completed.** Tell him you'll want to know if he can explain to someone who hasn't heard it before what the reading was mostly about. Briefly review what a good retelling includes—for example, describing elements of story grammar with a narrative and stating the main idea and details with an informational text.

✤ **Indicate where the child should begin reading, then record as he reads.** If the text is a short one, the reader will complete the whole selection. Allowing the child to read on in a longer selection will help him develop a stronger sense of the story line (or informational content) as well as the author's style. Reading accuracy generally improves when the reader has a chance to "get into" the text. For a chapter book or longer picture book, preselect a logical stopping place. Let the reader know that you'll be telling him when to stop, but don't say where in advance. Indicating the stopping point before the reading tends to cause readers to rush to that place.

✤ **When the child is finished reading, thank him, give one compliment, and ask for the retelling.** *You didn't rush this time. I like the expression you used. It was just right. Now tell me all about what you just read as if I were someone who never heard it before.* As the child retells, record your observations on the appropriate retelling assessment checklist.

✤ **Share highlights of the reading and retelling and, together, set goals.** *I noticed that you repeated here and here. When you reread, you corrected some errors that were causing confusion. I'm so glad that you're thinking along as you read and doing something to get back on track when you notice it doesn't make sense. That's what good readers do.*

This word, right here, is a word that you missed several times. I'll read the sentence out loud and see if that helps you think what the word must be. I'm sure you've heard the word and even used it yourself.

If the child still cannot identify the word, say it for him and explain its meaning. If the child identifies the word, ask him how he recognized it this time. In either case, follow up with: *What do you notice about it that will help you remember it next time?*

Continue with comments related to the retelling and look toward the next session. *The only things I had to remind you about in the retelling were the setting and connections you made or your ideas about it. You retold most of the events in the order that they happened. Let's talk about what you can practice before your next running record.*

✤ **Let the child know you enjoyed your time with him.** Be sure he clearly understands what to do once he gets back to his desk. *I can see how much you've grown and that you're using strategies comfortably now. Fixing up errors seemed harder for you before. I can tell you're really thinking about what you're reading as you go. Reviewing the retelling chart and practicing with a buddy is a good goal. When you get back to your desk, you can read by yourself. There's still some silent-reading time left.*

Completing the Record

After a running-record session, and while the class is still working independently, go over the records while they are fresh in your mind. Fill in any notations and observations that you want to include. Make sure your writing is legible. Clarify any shorthand now (I've sometimes forgotten what I meant due to overly abbreviated notations). Calculate percentages and analyze miscues later when the children are not in class). If you intend to have a child at the pre-primer level read another selection, go on without calculating a percentage.

When you've completed calculations, compare the overall score on the oral reading (word recognition) and the overall judgment of retelling competence (full, partial, fragmented) to the chart on the next page. Determine what level the text read falls into for this child.

Three Levels of Reading

	Word Recognition Accuracy (oral reading)	Retelling (comprehension)
Independent (I can read by myself.)	95-100%	full/complete
Instructional (I can read with help.)	90-94%	partial/satisfactory
Frustrational (It's too hard for me right now.)	below 90%	fragmented

Some examples:

If the child read *Art Lesson* by Tomie dePaola with 92% word recognition (oral reading) accuracy and a satisfactory retelling, that text would be at the child's instructional level. It would be an appropriate text for a teacher-supported literature study. If this child were a second grader, he would be working at grade level since *Art Lesson* has a grade-2 level of difficulty (Perma-Bound, 1999).

If the child read *Art Lesson* with 98% word recognition accuracy and retold it completely, the book would be at his independent level. It would be an appropriate book for silent-reading time.

If the child struggled with a 70% word recognition accuracy and a fragmented retelling, the text is at the child's frustrational level. If this child is a second grader, he would be reading slightly below grade level, since he struggled with a book at a grade-2 difficulty level.

If the scores for word reading accuracy and retelling do not both fall in a particular range ("Three Levels of Reading," above), use the "Split Levels of Performance" chart that follows to determine the overall level of the selection for this child.

The "Split Levels of Performance" chart will help you balance each part of the performance in order to determine the overall level of a text. Using the arrows to guide you, notice that if the child's oral reading is in the independent range (95-100%), but retelling is at the frustrational (fragmented) level, the selection is at her frustrational level overall. If oral reading is at the frustrational level (below 90%), but retelling is full and complete, the selection is at the instructional level overall.

Children who are transitioning to silent reading or who already do most of their reading silently may be less accurate in an oral performance even though they comprehend what they read. Some of these readers just get nervous when reading aloud and perform better on silent reading and retelling. Some readers who have a lot of background knowledge on a selec-

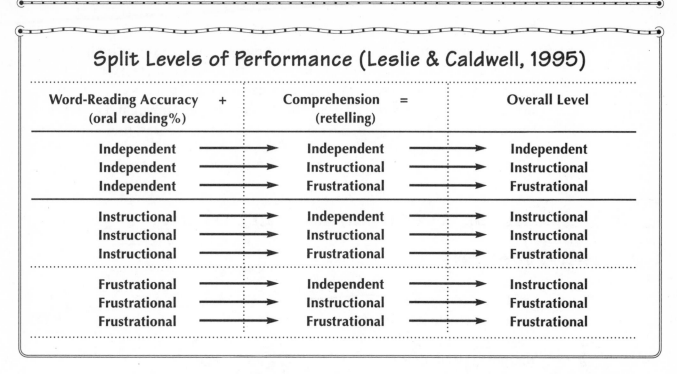

Split Levels of Performance (Leslie & Caldwell, 1995)

Word-Reading Accuracy + (oral reading%)	Comprehension = (retelling)	Overall Level
Independent →	Independent →	Independent
Independent →	Instructional →	Instructional
Independent →	Frustrational →	Frustrational
Instructional →	Independent →	Instructional
Instructional →	Instructional →	Instructional
Instructional →	Frustrational →	Frustrational
Frustrational →	Independent →	Instructional
Frustrational →	Instructional →	Frustrational
Frustrational →	Frustrational →	Frustrational

tion may over rely on what they already know to support comprehension and pay less attention to the details of the selection. When this happens they often miss new information and information that contradicts their prior knowledge. Many children can read more difficult narrative texts but have trouble with informational texts or texts on topics for which they have limited background knowledge.

Overall Performance Assessment

Many variables affect overall performance. Scores are greatly affected by the child's motivation to read a particular text, her background knowledge of the content, and its genre (narrative vs. informational). It is important to compare a child's reading across several running record assessments, as well as consider other evidence of literacy growth, before making overall determinations. Summative evaluations, used in reporting students' progress at scheduled times during an academic year, must integrate information from multiple situations. Running records of word-reading accuracy and standard retellings are important resources for writing overall evaluations. Useful information can be derived from each record or evaluation. However, other possible data sources include journal entries and responses in literature discussions. Minimally, documented information from three reading situations in which the child used specific skills (i.e., comprehension skills) should be included, since each made different demands on the reader and revealed a range of competencies with those skills. The "Continuous Skills Frame" (see pages 96–97 for primary- and intermediate-level frames) provides a scale to determine a reader's level of development based on a range of observed competencies.

Drawing from several types of assessment reinforces the principle that it's necessary to analyze multiple assessments from multiple sources and situations before making overall evaluations. Even when made, evaluations are never written in stone. They reflect a conclusion drawn at a given moment in time, based on the evidence at hand. Each day, new experiences and learning change the landscape.

Using Running Records as Part of an Overall Evaluation

Each record reveals a child's performance level with a particular genre of text, on a particular topic, at a particular level of difficulty. The following analyses (based on the running-records samples for Jamie, Sean, and Lisa), previously presented in this book, illustrate how the implications drawn from running records become an integral part of making an overall performance assessment.

Retelling Checklist—Narrative

Name _Jamie_____ Date_____

Text _Shadows Are About_____

Familiar/Unfamiliar _somewhat____ Background Information (full/limited) _personal experiences_

	Unassisted Retelling	Assisted Retelling	Illustrations Shown
Named main characters.	boy and girl		
Named other characters.		dog and cat	
Named setting (time/place).	at their house	outside, in the car, riding a bike	
Stated initiating event.	wake up and see shadows		
Identified problem.	kids are telling about all the kinds of shadows		
Described attempts to solve the problem.	they find all the shadows and make some		
Identified reaction of main character to attempts and solution of problem.	NA		
Retold story in correct sequence.			needed to look back, but sequence not critical
Made inferences related to the text.	It's a brother and sister. They're reading in bed		
Made connections with other texts or experience.	I made my shadow on my bike.	My dad can make shadow animals.	
Made evaluative statements about the writing, illustrations or story.		I like the pictures best 'cause I know about shadows but the pictures make the kids friendly. I liked the rabbit in the pictures.	

Level of Comprehension: _____ Full and detailed ✓ Partial/Satisfactory _____ Fragmented

Comments _Knows a lot about shadows — relying on prior knowledge._____

84   *Taking Running Records* Scholastic Professional Books

Running Record Recording Form

Reader _Jamie_____ Gr. _1_ Date _____ Recorder _____

Text Read _Shadows Are About_____ Familiar ✓ Unfamiliar ____ Genre _concept book_

Accuracy: _90_% SC: _3/3_ E freq: _every 10th word_ Reading rate: ___fast ✓ av. ___ slow Text level: _K-1_

Comprehension: ____ full ✓ satisfactory _____ fragmented or % ____ on questions asked

Comments _Used picture clues effectively. Several miscues maintained meaning — i.e. stand for stretch. Breaks up compound words with pause between — but not smooth. Uses strategy of covering up ½ of compound word, decoding each part, then blending. Not "stopping in tracks" with longer words now._____

Reading level for this text: ____ independent ✓ instructional _____ frustrational

Jamie: First grader Jamie read *Shadows Are About*. This text is at the pre-primer or grade K–1 level. As a concept book, it would be considered a *predictable* text since it is about a concept that is very familiar to most young children. Jamie read the book with 90% accuracy, which is in the instructional range. His retelling was assessed as partial/satisfactory, or instructional. Therefore, overall, this text is at Jamie's instructional level.

Instructional word reading + instructional comprehension = instructional level overall.

For guided reading, with the teacher helping him, it appears that informational books at a K–1 level would be appropriate for Jamie. He may be able to go higher. The ceiling (highest level he can go and still be instructional) has not been identified. If Jamie keeps reading more difficult books, the first level that is frustrational would establish a ceiling for his instructional levels. Just below that point is where the instructional level ends. Since Jamie is in first grade and a grade K–1 text is at his instructional level, he is performing at grade level.

Sean: Sean, a second grader, read *If You Traveled on the Underground Railroad*. This text is at a grade-3 level of difficulty (Perma-Bound, 1999). Sean's word-reading accuracy was 91%, or at the instructional level. His retelling was satisfactory, or instructional. Therefore, overall, this text is at Sean's instructional level.

Retelling Checklist—Informational Text

Name: Sean   Date: _____   Selection: If You Traveled on the Underground Railroad

THE STUDENT...	UNASSISTED RETELLING	ASSISTED RETELLING
1 Restates main idea	It's about when is it the best time to escape?	
2 Restates subtopic	It talks about why winter and summer are good.	
3 Identifies key terms/ vocabulary		
4 Identifies key people	the slaves	hunters, the slave hunters, owners of slaves
5 Makes inferences	summer is the best time, I think.	The owners wouldn't like to chase them in the winter. It's nasty weather for them too.
6 Recognizes cause & effect		If snow covers the trail, you can get lost.
7 Comprehends sequence of events/details/order of operation	It told why summer's a good time, then why winter is. Then it told about when it would be in the news-paper.	
8 Understands relative importance of subject matter	You'd have to figure this out carefully if you were a slave. you could die or get caught.	
9 Refers to and interprets visuals	NA	
10 Draws conclusions using prior knowledge and information from text		They were brave and wanted freedom real bad. I would too, but I'd be afraid of the hunters.

Level of Comprehension: _____ Full and detailed ✓ Partial _____ Fragmentary

Comments: Understood overall message — vague and/or Confused on details

Taking Running Records Scholastic Professional Books   81

Running Record Recording Form

Reader: Sean   Gr. _____ Date _____ Recorder _____

Text Read: If You Traveled on the Underground Railroad   Familiar _____ Unfamiliar _____ Genre: informational (he identified)

Accuracy: 91 % SC: 4/13 E freq: every 11th word Reading rate: ✓ fast ___ av. ___ slow Text level: Gr. 3

Comprehension: _____ full ✓ satisfactory _____ fragmented or % _____ on questions asked

Comments: Read very quickly — disregarded punctuation, especially commas. Substitutions were meaningful. Pace of reading likely contributed to omissions and dropped endings. Gained fluency after first paragraph. Could describe overall gist of the passage

Reading level for this text: _____ independent ✓ instructional _____ frustrational

Instructional word reading + instructional comprehension = instructional level overall.

For guided reading, with the teacher helping, it appears that informational books at a grade-3 level would be appropriate for Sean. He may be able to go higher. Since Sean is in grade 2 and a grade-3 text is at his instructional level, he is performing above grade level.

Lisa: Lisa, a third grader, read *Nana Upstairs, Nana Downstairs*. This text is at a grade-2 level of difficulty (Perma-Bound, 1999). Lisa's word-reading accuracy was 93%, or the instructional level. Her retelling was satisfactory, or instructional. Therefore, overall, this text is at Lisa's instructional level.

Comprehensive Rubric for Story Retellings

Name **Lisa** Date _____

Story **Nana Upstairs and Nana Downstairs** Rdg. Level: ___ Ind. ✓ Instr. ___ Frus.

Comprehension Elements	Score of 1	Score of 2	Score of 3	Score of 4
Story Grammar [4]	Even with prompting, reader is unable to state or confuses elements of story grammar.	With prompting, the reader includes most of the elements of story grammar ([]characters, []setting, []problem, []event sequence, []resolution)	Without prompting, reader includes most of the elements of story grammar ([]characters, []setting, []problem, []event sequence, []resolution)	Without prompting, reader includes all elements of story grammar ([✓]characters, [✓]setting, [✓]problem, [✓]event sequence, [✓]resolution) *NA*
Details [2]	Even with prompting, reader does not include or gives inaccurate details.	With prompting, reader includes some accurate details. *sketchy retelling — questioning brought out recall of details*	Without prompting, reader laces retelling with some significant & accurate details.	Without prompting, reader laces retelling with all significant & accurate details and some minor ones in a subordinate way.
Inferences, Predictions & Conclusions [2]	Even with prompting, reader does not convey understanding of or confuses story inferences, predictions, and/or conclusions.	With prompting, reader conveys understanding of story inferences, predictions, and/or conclusions. *inferences needed to be guided*	Without prompting, reader explains inferences, predictions, and/or conclusions drawn, however they are weak or minimal.	Without prompting, reader explains critical inferences, predictions, and/or conclusions drawn.
Connections to Reader's Life & Other Texts [3]	Even with prompting, reader is unable to make or confuses connections with other texts and/or life experiences.	With prompting, reader makes connections with other texts and/or life experiences.	Without prompting, reader explains connections with other texts and/or life experiences that vaguely relate to this text. *her one grandma is old and sick too*	Without prompting, reader explains connections with other texts and/or life experiences that closely relate to this text.
Type of Fictional Selection (specific genre) [3]	Even with prompting, reader is unable to identify type of fictional selection (i.e., fairy tale, fantasy, mystery, historical fiction, etc.).	With excessive prompting, reader identifies type of fictional selection (i.e., fairy tale, fantasy, mystery, historical fiction, etc.).	With limited prompting, reader identifies type of fictional selection s/he read (i.e., fairy tale, fantasy, mystery, historical fiction, etc.). *story is about his grandma when he was little (personal narrative)*	With limited prompting, reader identifies type of fictional selection s/he read (i.e., fairy tale, fantasy, mystery, historical fiction, etc.).

Comments **Lisa enjoyed the book. She made connections to visiting her grandma who is very ill. She said her grandma is sweet, like Tomie's.**

Taking Running Records Scholastic Professional Books   83

Running Record Recording Form

Reader **Lisa** Gr. **3** Date _____ Recorder _____

Text Read **Nana Upstairs, Nana Downstairs** Familiar ____ Unfamiliar ✓ Genre **narrative (she identified)**

Accuracy: **93**% SC: **7/15** E freq: **every 15th word** Reading rate: ____ fast ✓ av. ____ slow Text level: **Gr. 2**

Comprehension: ____ full ✓ satisfactory ____ fragmented or % ____ on questions asked

Comments **Errors did not generally interrupt meaning—most were insignificant differences (i.e. grandma for grandmother, stairs for stairway) reflecting her patterns of speech. Disregarded commas.**

Reading level for this text: ____ independent ✓ instructional ____ frustrational

Instructional word reading + instructional comprehension = instructional level overall.

For guided reading, with the teacher helping, it appears that narrative selections at a grade-2 level would be appropriate for Lisa. She may be able to go higher. Since Lisa is in grade 3 and a grade-2 text is at her instructional level, she is performing below grade level.

One More Thing ... Miscue Analysis

Most of the time, I'm able to determine how well a child is integrating cues (semantic, syntactic, or visual) as I review his completed running record, but sometimes I need a more detailed analysis. For example, I may need to know if the child is using meaning as the dominant cue system with syntactic and visual cues playing a supporting role. One final piece of the running record-miscue analysis—reveals more detail about the errors. It shows which cues the reader used efficiently and which he applied unsuccessfully or overlooked, creating a miscue (missed cue). Children's errors, or miscues, are windows to their thinking. Chapter 6 will focus on how to analyze miscues to detect patterns of cue use and misuse. It will also give hints for looking closer at the retelling.

Continuous Skills Frame for Literacy Development

PRIMARY LEVELS

	Early Emergent	Emergent	Beginning	Developing
1.	Identifies own name in print.	Is developing sight vocabulary.	Is increasing sight vocabulary to include content-area words.	Adjusts strategies to different reading material.
2.	Tells a story from pictures.	Reads simple books with repeated language patterns.	Reads books with growing confidence.	Identifies a variety of genres (i.e., biographies, nonfiction, poetry).
3.	Is aware that print carries the message.	Is beginning to use decoding strategies to identify words.	Is increasing and refining decoding skills.	Often reads chapter books.
4.	Can discuss a teacher-read story.	Is beginning to self-correct.	Applies cross-checking skills.	Applies multiple decoding strategies.
5.	Joins in with oral readings of familiar stories.	Is beginning to use basic comprehension strategies (i.e., sequence, inference, drawing conclusions, predicting).	Selects books of interest based on topic and/or author.	Refines cross-checking strategies to self-correct.
6.	Retells familiar story in own words.	Self-selects books for reading.	Uses basic comprehension strategies more independently.	Applies multiple strategies more independently and at the appropriate time to comprehend text.
7.	Shows curiosity about print.	Is aware of types of literature.	Is confident when talking about books with others.	Reads aloud with expression and appropriate pauses.
8.	Is developing a sense of wordness.	Maintains independent reading for a short time—initially about 5 minutes.	Shows familiarity with several titles, authors, and illustrators introduced at the child's level.	Attends to silent reading for an extended period of time—initially about 15 minutes.
9.	Recognizes letters of the alphabet.	Understands fundamental concepts of print (i.e., sentence punctuation such as periods, question and quotation marks.	Maintains independent reading for a minimum of 10 minutes.	Often chooses books at appropriate level for personal reading.
10.	Recognizes that letters carry sound.		Is beginnning to apply understanding of concepts of print in oral reading.	
11.	Shows interest in books.			
12.	Is aware of concepts of print, (i.e., directionality, book format).			

(Adapted from *The Primary Language Record*, 1989; LA Portfolio Handbook Juneau School District, 1992; NYSED—Early Literacy Profile, 1999)

Name _____ Date _____

Continuous Skills Frame for Literacy Development
INTERMEDIATE LEVELS

	Guided	Independent	Expanded Independent
1.	Develops further understanding of print (i.e., punctuation such as question marks, quotation marks) in order to read expressively, applying punctuation to indicate meaning.	Uses independent action to solve reading problems.	Establishes criteria to judge/ evaluate a piece of literature.
2.	Reads known and predictable books with growing confidence, but still needs support with new and unfamiliar ones.	Reads independently, using concepts of print without guidance.	Verifies information to prove or disprove a view associated with a piece of literature.
3.	Increasingly uses meaning, language, and print cues to read.	Uses meaning, language, and print cues in reading independently.	Considers alternatives to open-ended questions.
4.	Is very familiar with several titles, authors, styles, and illustrators introduced at this level (able to identify each area).	Paraphrases the main idea of a piece of writing in any curricular area.	Selects from a variety of genres or personal reading.
5.	Predicts what might happen given a lead-in.	Chooses books for personal reading at an appropriate level.	Uses decoding skills independently.
6.	Infers (draws conclusions) based on material read.	Uses appropriate self-correction skills.	Critically analyzes/evaluates selections for validity of information.
7.	Identifies main idea and supporting details in literature and across all content areas.	Uses refined comprehension strategies associated with interpreting characters, language, text style.	Uses a wide variety of reference materials independently.
8.	Is becoming more comfortable in using comprehension strategies with guidance (i.e., interpreting elements of characterization, figurative language, point of view, genre structure).	Expands use of decoding skills.	Makes connections with new reading to prior reading, background knowledge and current events in the world.
9.	Uses decoding skills to increase word recognition.	Expands use of reference materials (i.e., dictionary, thesaurus).	Makes personal connections through reading (grows cognitively, socially, and/or emotionally).

CHAPTER 6

Looking Closer

Now, following the initial calculations and evaluations in the running record, it's time to fine tune your thinking with a closer analysis of the child's miscues and retellings. Careful scrutiny of individual items can help you plan follow-up and direct instruction and set long term goals for your students. Teaching guided by detailed assessment information that detects problems and captures teachable moments moves learners forward.

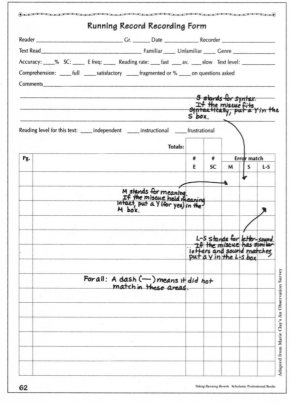

Analyzing Miscues

Return to the running record form and study, line by line, substitution miscues (incorrect word errors) in relationship to their immediate context (sentence and paragraph) as well as the passage as a whole (overall theme of the passage). Determine whether the miscue is appropriate for meaning (it doesn't impede comprehension—i.e., a synonym), appropriate for syntax (grammar or language structure—i.e., similar part of speech, same verb tense, or same number—singular or plural) or has a degree of letter-sound match. To represent these types of miscues on your running record, you'll use M, S, and L-S respectively, in the error match column. There may be debate about shades of differences with meaning appropriateness. Use your best judgment. Be "tight" on syntactic appropriateness. Noticing variations in word forms is important for distinguishing exact meaning as well as spelling and writing development.

Meaning-Appropriate Miscues

Meaning-appropriate (M column) substitutions make sense and do not interrupt the general comprehension of the sentence, paragraph, or pas-

Reader	Text	Error Match		
		M	S	L-S
forest	cave	Y	Y	—
wild	cave	Y	Y	—
woods	cave	Y	Y	—

sage. M miscues may be syntactically appropriate, but may not have a letter-sound correlation. Often, these are synonyms or additions that may even enhance clarity. For example, in the sentence, *Bears live in the _____.*, the child may read *forest, wild,* or *woods* for *cave* after referring to picture clues. These would not interrupt meaning and would be syntactically appropriate. However, none of these miscues incorporate a letter-sound match.

Syntactically Appropriate Miscues

Reader	Text	Error Match		
		M	S	L-S
cart	cave	—	Y	Y
call	cave	—	—	Y
cage	cave	Y	Y	Y

Syntactically appropriate (S) substitutions keep sentence structure intact, though they may or may not keep meaning intact. For example, a child may come up with *cart* when the word is *cave*. In this case, it has a letter-sound match; it is a thing or place, but it doesn't make sense. The reader is applying what he knows about how the language goes together and what *kind* of word belongs in this place. Young children know, for example, that a describing word or a naming word (the name of the part of speech is not important at this point) would come next in the sentence, *Bears live in the _____*, because they've heard the language and use it to communicate. The child is using letter-sound and language structure knowledge to take a stab at the word, but is not cross-checking for meaning by applying the self-monitoring question: *Does the word I'm saying make sense in this place?* If the child was only using letter-sound information and not syntax, he might have said, *Bears live in the* call. If he was using all cueing systems—meaning, syntax, and letter-sound—he might have said *cage* (like bears in the zoo) as a miscue. Hopefully, the child would have read on and realized that *cage* would not be appropriate if these bears were in the wild. Good readers stop when meaning is interrupted and go back to reread and apply fix-up strategies.

Letter-Sound Match Miscues

Reader	Text	Error Match		
		M	S	L-S
home	house	Y	Y	Y
whale	wheel	—	Y	Y

Letter-sound match (L-S) substitutions refer to similarity in letters and sounds between the miscue and the word in the text. As shown previously, miscues matching in L-S may or may not be meaningful or syntactically appropriate. For example, *home* for *house* would match in L-S to some degree and be meaning and syntactically appropriate in most cases. However, *whale* for *wheel* would likely not be meaning appropriate although there is a L-S match and it is the same part of speech (S). Some L-S matches may be very minimal—only a beginning sound similarity, but closely resemble the size and shape of the text word.

Significant and Insignificant Miscues

Miscues that inhibit a child's understanding of a text and diminish his reading fluency are considered to be significant. Comprehension quickly becomes fragmented when decoding lacks smoothness, automaticity, and reasonable accuracy. Miscues that do not interrupt overall understanding of a passage are considered insignificant. However, if a child makes many insignificant miscues, there's a risk that he's altering or misinterpreting the author's message. An error that matches all three cue systems would most likely be an insignificant miscue.

Miscue Patterns

The analysis of one running record will not be conclusive, but studying several may create a distinct pattern of how the child uses, misuses, and overuses cues. Analyzing a reader's pattern of miscues can help you plan instruction that reinforces developing skills, introduces new skills when readers are ready, and emphasizes the balanced, well orchestrated use of the cueing systems. Just as the musical conductor knows when to bring in the strings, when to bring in the percussion instruments, and how to blend all the sounds as he directs the symphony, efficient readers employ appropriate cue systems as they smoothly navigate text.

Miscues made with frustrational level text generally fall in the letter-sound category because at that level, the child cannot read fluently enough to apply meaning and language-structure (syntactic) clues. Consequently, miscues made on frustrational text should be used cautiously in miscue analysis, if at all.

If the reader's miscues are predominately meaning and syntactically appropriate, she is focused on understanding and getting the gist of the passage. Good readers make these kinds of miscues as they read to maintain the flow of comprehension. They'll use a synonym and look up the text word later. Encourage readers to inquire about the new words in order to enlarge their reading, writing, listening, and speaking vocabularies. Sometimes the reader has to stop, look up word (a technical term for example), or ask for help in order to grasp a concept that is central to understanding the passage. This is especially common with informational texts.

Often, young children with extensive oral language vocabularies make miscues that improve a very simple text. They insert words and phrases that are in their speaking vocabularies, but too complex for use in an emergent level text. In such a case, a child's word-reading accuracy may be low, while his comprehension is very high. If children habitually use meaning and syntax substitutions it can be problematic. At times when the reader's miscues do change the author's message, subtly or dramatically, he can become confused and misinterpret the author's point or draw false conclusions.

Sample Miscue Analyses

Review the running records for Sean, Lisa, and Jamie introduced in chapter 3 but included here with the miscue analysis completed. Following each, I've analyzed the miscue substitutions. Teacher given words (T), counted as errors, are not analyzed.

Sample Running Record

Sean, reading *If You Traveled on the Underground Railroad*

Page	Text	Sean's Reading
pg. 47	When was the best time of year to escape?	When was the best time of year to escape?
	Some people said summer, some said winter.	Some people said summer some said winter.
	If you traveled in summer, you didn't have to worry	If you travel in summer you didn't have to wor..
	about the cold. The trees were green, and there were	about the cold—worry about the cold. The trees were green and there was
	lots of berries and small animals for food. But it was	a lot of berries and small animals to find for food. But it was
	also easier for the hunters to follow you.	also easy for the hunters to find you.
	Winter, of course, could be bitter cold. But there	Winter, of c..c.cuz could be cold. But that
	were good reasons for going then. The rivers were	was good reason—reasons—for going then. The rivers were
	often frozen. You could cross them by walking on the	often. You could cross them by walking on the
	ice. In the summer you might have to find a boat.	ice. In the summer you might have to find a boat.
	Many slaves ran away at Christmas. Their owners	Many slaves ran away at Christmas. Their owners
	were so busy going to parties, they might not notice	were busy going to parties, they might not notice
	for several days that a slave was missing. That would	for several days that a slave was missing. That would
	give you a head start.	give you a head start.
	Whether it was summer or winter, certain days	When it was summer or winter cer—days
	were better than others for your escape. Saturday was	were better—some days were better—than others for your escape. Saturday was
	best. The newspapers wouldn't print advertisements	best. The news... newspapers wouldn't write ad-ver..stories
	on Sunday. And so the owners couldn't tell everyone	on Sunday. And so the owners couldn't tell everyone
	that you had run off. That also gave you a head start.	that you had run off. That also gave you a head start.
pg. 48	And whether it was summer or winter, you hoped	And when it was summer or winter, you hoped
	for clear nights. Then you could look up at the sky	for clear nights. Then you could look up at the sky
	and follow the North Star. It pointed toward freedom.	and follow the North Star. It pointed towards freedom.

Taking Running Records Scholastic Professional Books

Pg.		# E	# SC	Error match M	S	L-S
47	✓✓✓✓✓✓✓✓					
	✓✓✓✓ Ⓞ ✓✓✓ ᴿᶜ					
	✓✓ travel/traveled ✓✓ Ⓞ ✓✓✓✓ was/worry	1	1	Y	–	Y
	✓✓ ᴿ ✓✓✓✓ Ⓞ ✓✓ was/were	1		Y	–	Y
	a lot/Tots ✓✓✓✓ to/se find/for food/R ✓✓✓	2	2	Y	–	Y
	easy/easier ✓ ✓✓✓ find/follow ✓	2		Y	=	Y
	c...cuz/course ✓✓ bitter ✓✓ that/there	3		Y	Y	Y
	was/Were ✓ reason ˢᶜ/reasons ✓✓✓✓✓	1	1	Y	–	Y
	✓ frozen ✓✓✓✓✓✓✓	1				
	✓✓✓✓✓✓✓✓✓					
	✓✓✓✓✓✓✓					
	✓ 50 ✓✓✓✓✓✓✓	1				
	✓✓✓✓✓✓✓✓ ✓✓					
	✓✓✓✓✓					
	when/Whether ✓✓✓✓ Ⓞ some/her/certain ✓	2		Y	=	Y
	✓✓ ᴿ ✓✓✓✓✓ stories					
	✓✓ news.../newspapers ✓ write/print at-ver/advertisements	2		Y	Y	=
	✓✓✓✓✓✓✓✓					
	✓✓✓✓✓✓✓✓✓✓					
48	✓ when/whether ✓✓✓✓ ✓✓	1		Y	–	Y
	✓✓✓✓✓✓✓✓✓					
	✓✓✓✓ ✓✓ towards/toward ✓	1		Y	Y	Y

18   4

$$\text{accuracy} = \frac{182}{200} = 91\%$$

$$\text{E freq.:} = \frac{200}{18} = 11 = \text{an error on every 11th word}$$

$$\text{SC freq.:} = \frac{4}{18} = \text{4 errors corrected and 18 left uncorrected}$$

Analyzing Substitution Miscues
SEAN

If You Traveled on the Underground Railroad

Y = yes: word is appropriate or a *match*   — = negative: word is not *appropriate* or a *match*

Miscue	Text Word	Error Match			Comment
		M	**S**	**L-S**	
travel	traveled	Y	—	Y	verb tense change
was	were	Y	—	Y	form for singular subject
lot	lots	Y	—	Y	read singular form to match insertion of *a*
easy	easier	Y	—	Y	ending omitted
find	follow	Y	Y	Y	
cuz	course	—	—	Y	nonword—slang for *because*
that	there	Y	Y	Y	
when	whether	Y	—	Y	
some	certain	Y	Y	—	
write	print	Y	Y	—	
stories	advertisements	—	Y	—	attempt to be meaningful but inaccurate in specifics
toward	towards	Y	Y	Y	common speech error

Sean is self-monitoring for meaning and applying letter-sound knowledge. One miscue that was not syntactically appropriate was caused by his effort to make another miscue fit. After inserting the word *a*, he read *lots* as a singular word—*lot*. He has difficulty discriminating the high frequency words—*was, were, that, there,* and *when*. He dropped endings as well—*travel* for *traveled* and *easy* for *easier*. He gave a meaningful substitution, *write* for *print* (*The newspapers wouldn't print*). The miscue *stories* for *advertisements* was an attempt at meaning. Sean got the gist of the paragraph, but this is a case of specifics that affect the accuracy of comprehension. The newspapers did print *stories*, but not *advertisements* for lost slaves on Sunday.

Taking Running Records Scholastic Professional Books

Sample Running Record: Lisa, reading Nana Upstairs & Nana Downstairs

Page	Text	Lisa's Reading
pg. 1	When Tommy was a little boy, he had a grandmother and a great-grandmother. He loved both of them very much.	When Tommy was a little boy he had a grandmother and a great-grandmother He loved both of them very much.
pg 2	He and his family would go to visit every Sunday afternoon. His grandmother always seemed to be standing by the big black stove in the kitchen.	He and his family would go to visit on Sunday........ His grandma always seemed/see to be standing/st stand R by the big black stove in the kitchen.
pg. 3	His great-grandmother was always in bed upstairs because she was ninety-four years old. So Tommy called them Nana Downstairs and Nana Upstairs.	His great-grandma was always in bed upstairs/up-stairs because she was ...ninety...four R years old. So Tommy called them Nana.....Downstairs and Nana Upstairs.
pg. 4	Almost every Sunday was the same. Tommy would run into the house, say hello to his Grandfather Tom, and Nana Downstairs and then go up the back stairway to the bedroom where Nana Upstairs was.	Almost every Sunday was the same Tommy would run into the house and say hello to his Grandpa Tom and Nana .... Downstairs and then go up the back stairs to the bedroom where Nana Upstairs was.
pg. 5	"Get some candy," Nana Upstairs would say. And he would open the lid of the sewing box on the dresser, and there would be candy mints.	"Get some candy," Nana Upstairs would say. And he would open the lid/cover of the sewing box on the bureau and there would be candies. R
pg. 6	Once Nana Downstairs came into the bedroom and helped Nana Upstairs to the big Morris chair and tied her in so she wouldn't fall out. "Why will Nana Upstairs fall out?" Tommy asked. "Because she is ninety-four years old," Nana Downstairs said. "I'm four years old," Tommy said. "Tie me in a chair too!"	Once Nana Downstairs came into the bedroom and helped Nana Upstairs to the big Man's chair and tied/tried her in so she wouldn't fall out. "Why will Nana Upstairs fall out?" Tommy asked. "Because she is ninety-four years old," Nana Downstairs said. "I'm four years old," Tommy said. "Tie me in a chair too!"
pg. 7	So every Sunday, after he found the candy mints in the sewing box on the dresser, Nana Downstairs would come up the back stairway and tie Nana Upstairs and Tommy in their chairs, and then they would eat their candy and talk.	So every Sunday, after he found the candy mints/candies...... in the sewing box on the s..dresser/dress...., Nana Downstairs would come up the back stairs and tie Nana Upstairs and Tommy in their chairs, and then they would eat their candies and talk.

Pg.		# E	# SC	Error match M	S	L-S
1	✓✓✓✓✓✓ ⓢ ✓✓					
	✓✓✓✓✓ ✓					
	✓✓✓✓✓✓					
2	✓✓✓✓✓✓✓					
	on/Every ✓ H (afternoon) ✓ grandma/grandmother 3			Y̲/Y	─̲/Y	─̲/Y
	✓ se se/seemed ✓✓ st-stand-R/standing H ✓✓		2			
	✓✓✓✓✓					
3	✓✓ grandma/grandmother ✓✓ ✓	1		Y	Y	Y
	✓ up-stairs ✓/upstairs ✓✓✓H✓H✓R					
	✓✓					
	✓✓✓✓ H ✓					
	✓✓✓					
4	✓✓✓ ✓ ✓					
	✓✓✓ ✓ ✓✓ ⓢ^and ✓	1				
	✓✓✓ grandpa/grand-father ✓ⓢ ✓✓	1		Y	Y	Y
	H ✓✓ ✓✓✓✓					
	stairs/stairway ✓✓✓✓	1		Y	Y	Y
	✓✓					
5	✓✓ ✓✓ ✓ ✓					
	✓✓✓✓✓✓ sc cover/lid ✓		1			
	✓ st sc (Sewing box) R ✓ bureau/dresser ✓✓	1	2	Y	Y	─
	✓✓ candies/candy (mints)	2		Y	─	Y
6	✓✓ ✓ ✓✓					
	✓✓ ✓✓ ✓✓					
	✓ Man's/Morris ✓✓ tried se/fied ✓✓✓	1	1	─	─	Y
	✓✓✓					
	✓✓✓✓✓					
	✓✓					
	✓✓✓✓✓					
	✓✓✓✓					
	✓✓✓✓					
7	✓✓✓✓✓✓					
	candies se A-T/Candy (mints) R ✓✓✓✓✓✓	1	1			
	dress A-T/dresser ✓✓✓✓ ✓	1				
	✓✓ stairs/stairway ✓✓✓✓	1		Y	Y	Y
	✓✓✓✓✓✓					
	✓✓✓ candies/Candy ✓✓	1		Y	─	Y
		15	**7**			

$$\text{accuracy} = \frac{214}{229} = 93\%$$

$$\text{E freq.}: = \frac{214}{15} = 15 = \text{an error every 15th word}$$

$$\text{SC freq.}: = \frac{7}{15} = 7 \text{ corrected errors and 15 left uncorrected}$$

Taking Running Records Scholastic Professional Books

Analyzing Substitution Miscues
LISA

Nana Upstairs & Nana Downstairs

Y = yes: word is appropriate or a *match*   — = negative: word is not *appropriate* or a *match*

Miscue	Text Word	Error Match			Comment
		M	**S**	**L-S**	
on	every	Y	—	—	
grandma	grandmother	Y	Y	Y	
grandpa	grandfather	Y	Y	Y	
stairs	stairway	Y	Y	Y	
bureau	dresser	Y	Y	—	used picture clue
candies	candy	Y	—	Y	plural for singular
Man's	Morris	—	—	Y	minimal match

Lisa repeated some miscues, maintaining identification for words that were more common forms in her speaking vocabulary. For example, she read *stairs* for *stairways*, *grandma* for *grandmother*, *grandpa* for *grandfather*, and *candies* for *candy mints*. Lisa also used picture clues as shown in her miscue—*bureau* for *dresser*. Most miscues were meaningful and integrated letter-sound knowledge.

Sample Running Record
Jamie, reading *Shadows Are About*

Page	Text	Jamie's Reading
pg. 1	It is day. The sun is out.	It is day. The sun is out.
pg. 3	Inside, outside, shadows are about.	In...side, out...side shadows are around.
pg. 5	They drive with cars and sway with trees.	They drive with cars and swing with trees.
pg. 7	They droop with flowers and fall with leaves.	They drop with flowers and fall with leaves.
pg. 9	They stretch with cats and chase with dogs.	They stand with cats and ch..ch..run with dogs.
pg. 10	They swim with ducks and jump with frogs.	They swim with ducks and jump with frogs.
pg. 12	Shadows run. Shadows skip.	Shadows run. Shadows sk...sk..ip.
pg. 13	Sometimes shadows turn a flip.	Some....times they do a flip.
pg. 14	They flap with flags…	They fly with flags...
pg. 15	…and swoop with kites.	...and swing with kites.
pg. 16	They roll with hoops…	They roll with hoops ...
pg. 17	…and race with bikes.	... and race with bikes.
pg. 18	Shadows hop. Shadows stand.	Shadows hop. Shadows stand.
	Shadows march beside a band.	Shadows m...m...march beside a band.
pg. 20	Late-day shadows stretch through rooms.	Long-day shadows start the rooms
	They sit with chairs and lean with brooms.	They sit with.... chairs and l..e..an lean with brooms
pg. 22	Shadows climb up and down.	Shadows climb up and down.
pg. 23	Shadows bounce around…around.	Shadows jump bounce around... around.
pg. 24	They clap with hands and roll with balls.	They clap with hands and roll with balls.
	They paint dark pictures on the walls.	They pain paint d..ark dark p..pic pictures on the walls.
pg. 26	But when the day turns into night…	But when the day ..turns... into night...
pg. 28	…shadows never stay…without a light.	...shadows never stay.. with..out without a light.

Taking Running Records Scholastic Professional Books

Pg.		# E	# SC	Error match M	S	L-S
1	✓✓ ✓ ✓ ✓ ✓					
3	in...side ✓ out...side ✓ ✓✓ around / Inside outside about	1		Y	Y	Y
5	✓✓✓✓ swing / away ✓✓	1		Y	Y	Y
7	✓ drop / droop ✓✓✓ ✓✓	1		—	Y	Y
9	✓ stand / stretch ✓✓✓ ch..d..run / chase ✓✓	2		Y Y	Y Y	Y —
10	✓✓ ✓✓ ✓✓ ✓					
12	✓✓ ✓ sk...sk..ip ✓ / SKIP					
13	some...times ✓ ✓ do⟨turn⟩ ✓✓ R / sometimes	1		Y	Y	—
14	✓ fly / flap ✓✓	1		Y	Y	Y
15	✓ swing / swoop ✓✓	1		Y	Y	Y
16	✓✓ ✓ ✓					
17	✓✓ ✓					
18	✓✓ ✓					
20	✓ m..m...A..T be-side ✓ ✓✓ / march beside	1			Y	Y
20	Long ✓✓ start the ✓ / Late stretch through	3		— —	Y Y	Y Y
	✓✓✓ H ✓✓ ✓ tr..s..an se ✓✓ / lean R		1			
22	✓✓ ✓ ✓ ✓					
23	✓ jump sc / bounce ✓✓		1			
24	✓ ✓ ✓ ✓ ✓ ✓ ✓					
26	✓ pain sc d..ark ✓ p..pie..✓ ✓✓✓ / paint dark pictures		1			
26	✓✓ ✓✓ A..T⟨turns⟩...✓✓	1				
28	✓✓✓ with..out ✓ ✓✓ / without					

13   3

$$accuracy = \frac{116}{129} = 89.9 = 90\%$$

$$E\ freq.: \frac{129}{13} = 9.9 = 10 = an\ error\ every\ 10th\ word$$

$$SC\ freq.: \frac{3}{13} = 3\ corrected\ errors\ and\ 13\ left\ uncorrected$$

Analyzing Substitution Miscues

JAMIE

Shadows Are About

Y = yes: word is appropriate or a *match*   **—** = negative: word is not *appropriate* or a *match*

Miscue	Text Word	Error Match			Comment
		M	**S**	**L-S**	
around	about	Y	Y	Y	minimal L-S
swing	sway	Y	Y	Y	used picture clue
drop	droop	—	Y	Y	used picture clue
stand	stretch	Y	Y	Y	picture for meaning
run	chase	Y	Y	—	used picture clue
do	turn	Y	Y	—	
fly	flap	Y	Y	Y	
swing	swoop	Y	Y	Y	used picture clue
long	late	—	Y	Y	
start	stretch	—	Y	Y	minimal L-S
the	through	—	—	Y	very minimal L-S

Jamie is reading for meaning. He's used picture clues and prior knowledge to generate sensible choices for new words, while frequently integrating letter-sound knowledge in the process. His strong use of picture clues indicates that he has learned how to use illustrations effectively as a support. This is an important strategy for emergent readers. Quality literature has illustrations that are designed to add appeal as well as clues to the print on the page. He is also using his knowledge of language structure to come up with words that have a grammatical fit. Jamie is integrating, or orchestrating, the cueing systems successfully.

Sample Retelling Analyses

To further examine the child's retelling abilities, look back at the retelling checklist to review when and how you had to prompt the child. As a general rule, prompting indicates that the text was at the reader's instructional level, since he needed assistance in recall, interpretations, and/or making connections. A cautionary note (or caveat) would be that the reader may be able to fully retell but is not yet comfortable with retelling expectations. The child may be so used to answering questions that he gives minimal answers and waits for prompts. It is very important to *model, model, model* retelling and *practice, practice, practice* the process, making expectations crystal clear.

Samples of Retelling Analysis

Sean (see page 93 for his retelling checklist)

If You Traveled on the Underground Railroad—**unfamiliar text. (Trade books, since they are available in libraries and bookstores, will never be "secure" in the way that IRI—Informal Reading Inventories—passages are. However, Sean did not recall having ever read or heard this book.)**

Sean understood the overall premise of the passage—that when to run away was a life or death decision for the slaves, and that there were advantages and disadvantages for summer and winter. He needed some prompting to expand on descriptions of other people involved in this situation, the cause and effect (effect of snow on trails) example in the passage, and personal inferences and feelings. Sean was fully engaged throughout the reading. He has shown keen interest in the topic of slavery and the Underground Railroad's connection to local history.

Jamie (see page 92 for his retelling checklist)

Shadows Are About—**familiar text. (The book had been used as a read-aloud, but Jamie hadn't read it before.)**

Jamie was very familiar with the concept of shadows and had engaged in activities much like those described in the book. He expressed these connections to personal experiences: *I raced my shadow on my bike.* With a prompt he added: *My dad can make shadow animals.*

He was able to retell elements of the story grammar that focused on names, other characters, and additional settings with minimal prompts. He didn't talk about characters' activities in the order they were presented in the text, but sequence was not essential for understanding. Prompts did not stimulate recall of additional events, but, with a review of illustrations, he did remember others. He noted the examples of experimenting with shadow movements that were similar to his own and glossed over those that were different or that he hadn't tried. It was here that he needed prompting. Jamie's evaluation of the text focused on an appreciation of the illustrations. This was typical, since Jamie is a budding first-grade artist with exceptional talent. Illustrations in his journal are always detailed.

Lisa (see page 94 for her retelling checklist)
***Nana Upstairs & Nana Downstairs*—unfamiliar text.**

Lisa moved swiftly through the elements of story grammar. She clearly understands this part of the task. She still depends on questioning to elaborate and make inferences. She needs help in identifying significant details and in shaping the expression of her inferences and predictions. A mini-lesson on this part of the retelling process has been planned for Lisa and a few others. She'll be practicing with a buddy at the end of silent-reading time. Lisa demonstrated how much she enjoyed the book during the reading and through comments about how Tomie's Nana is so much like her own. Lisa's mother has worked since she was a baby, and her Grandma has always been her regular babysitter. Lisa's Grandma was recently hospitalized, and Lisa is very concerned.

CHAPTER 7

Using Running Records to Inform Your Teaching

The information you elicit as you take running records and evaluate them is invaluable in planning how you will teach literacy skills. You can use the information to plan mini-(or longer) lessons for small groups or the whole class. In the process of developing *your* skills in using running records, you're constantly helping children improve their decoding and comprehension.

Ways Running Records Support Teaching

Teacher-Student Debriefing Conferences

These one-on-one interactions after the RR session provide a great opportunity for intense, individualized instruction. I've always found that I can accomplish a great deal of teaching in a very short time during these sessions.

For example, when I recognize that a reader has made a number of miscues that don't make sense, our conversation would start something like this:

Teacher: I was confused when you read this part. It sounded like you said____. Did that make sense to you?

Child: No.

T: If we want to know exactly how the slaves got help, we need to do some fixing. Don't you think?

C: Yes.

T: What can you do to help us understand what the author's saying?

C: Read it again.

T: Sure. It isn't working right now. We're confused and we still don't know how the conductors worked on the Underground Railroad. We should have gotten that answer in this part.

C: (rereads section) Now I get it. They .... That's how they got them from one stop to the next.

T: Good job! When it doesn't make sense to you, you want to remember to stop and figure out the problem so you'll understand what the author is saying. When you just keep going, it gets more and more confusing. You want it to make sense. Carefully rereading the confusing part is a good strategy.

When you and the reader have each other's undivided attention, concentration intensifies. And when the child *needs* to know something, he's motivated, and learning is more assured. You—or the child—may identify a need-to-know during a debriefing conference. I'd compare it to having a flat tire. If I were by the side of the road with a flat tire (but without an Automobile Policy from AAA), I'd need to know how to fix it. I'd concentrate hard on your explanation or the directions in a manual. However, if I weren't in that dire situation and had to read the car manual, my attention would be a lot less focused. Connecting a need or desire to know to your instruction creates the teachable moment.

Small-Group Lessons

Running records can help you group children with similar needs for instruction. Membership in these groups continuously changes according to students' needs for practice or readiness to learn a new skill.

For example, a number of readers may be making substitutions that keep the meaning intact, but begin to alter or blur the author's message. An ad hoc group would be formed to discuss why and how a reader should quickly confirm or correct his thinking after predicting what an unknown word might be. When you notice that some children are misusing or overusing substitutions, your small-group objective would be to draw the children's attention to the author's words. Explain that the strategy they are using can be very helpful, but can also cause problems. Ask a member of the group if you can use one of his miscues as an example for others. Then, discuss a particular error with that child as the others listen.

Teacher: Here, you said, *And they knew they could be put in prison for helping* people, *or even killed. But they helped anyway* (If You Traveled on the Underground Railroad). Let's look at the author's word. Does it have the letters you'd expect to see for the word *people*? Does it look like *people*?

Child: No.

T: It has *f-u-g-i-t-i-v-e.* This is a word that we met in our social studies book, and we talked about it. It means someone who is escaping from the law. Slaves were labeled with this term because a law said that they could not run away. People who thought that the law was unjust helped them anyway. Would someone be put in jail just for helping another person?

C: No.

T: Then, that can't be right, can it? That's another red flag telling you to look again. They wouldn't be put in prison just for helping people—any people, but they could be for helping people who were running away from the law. The author's word starts like *funeral*—/fū/, then a *g* before *i* that makes a /j/ sound for **/ j i /**, and, finally, *t-i-v-e* like the end of ac*tive*. It's /fū/—/j ĭ/— can you finish it?

(Note that making as many comparisons as possible to known words helps the reader begin to realize how the analogy strategy aids word recognition (decoding) when reading and spelling (encoding).

C: /Fu/—/ji/— *fugitive.*

T: That's it. Now the author's statement is clear. The Quakers were bravely putting themselves in danger of arrest for helping slaves who were *fugitives*, not simply for helping *people*. When we read on, we'll find out how a law freed the slaves.

Mini-Lessons Based on Oral-Reading Performances

The oral reading part of complete Running Records is replete with possibilities for future whole-class mini-lessons. Here are a few areas for effective lessons.

- ❊ **Skills and strategies for decoding.** Patterns of cueing systems used, confused, or overused point out skills that need to be taught and/or reinforced. For example, after making several miscues that were not meaningful, children might need instruction on how to use context clues to figure out unknown words.

- ❊ **Vocabulary development.** Performances may reflect limited vocabulary knowledge. Words that are not in children's speaking and listening vocabulary are more difficult to decode. Vocabulary lessons would support improvement in reading.

- ❊ **Models of fluency.** Fluency, measured by the number of words read before a miscue interrupts the flow, is a factor that affects comprehension. Limited fluency (only a few words read before a miscue interrupts) makes it difficult for readers to concentrate on processing information from the text. Teacher read-alouds help readers understand how reading should sound. Rereading a text (or sections of text), to make it sound like talking, helps readers experience the *feel* of fluency. Activities such as readers' theater create a purpose for rereading that results in increased fluency and appropriate expression.

❋ **Self-monitoring of miscues.** Do the children attempt to self-correct, recognizing that meaning has been lost? Are these attempts successful? How frequently do they self-correct—most or not many miscues? Modeling of self-correcting in read-alouds reinforces the concept that this is a strategy good readers—even adults—use. Discussion of ways that particular miscues could have been corrected provides specific how-tos for the process.

❋ Dropped endings or miscues related to structural changes in base words suggest mini-lessons on meaningful units in words and how these affect spelling and pronunciation.

❋ Miscues that indicate a lack of attention to medial sounds suggest mini-lessons on vowels and vowel patterns.

Mini-Lessons Based on Retelling Results

Retellings reflect children's ability to identify genres of writing, recognize elements of story grammar, accurately recall main ideas and details, integrate information with prior knowledge, make inferences and logical predictions, draw conclusions, and think creatively and critically about the content and presentation in the text. Needs in any of these micro or macro aspects of comprehension can become the seed for direct instruction in follow-up lessons.

You've introduced, modeled, and guided practice with these comprehension strategies, giving readers a repertoire of tools for the task. Plan mini-lessons in which you (or students) model how to retell in a way that presents information clearly and concisely with a sprinkling of personal connections and interpretations. Provide ample time for practice before expecting children to transfer strategies to independent use. Children's ability to use the retelling process as a vehicle for showing their knowledge has to be developed and refined.

Practice Together! Learn More!

After working with colleagues to analyze miscues and retellings in running records that you've taken, discuss possibilities for follow-up lessons that would reinforce strengths and ameliorate problems identified in individual samples. Establish groups to plan specific instruction for various lessons.

Targeting Individual Needs

With the data you derive from running records, you can quantify a child's overall success as well as analyze the nature of the mistakes she makes in each reading. Instruction that flows from reflecting on running-record calculations and conclusions targets individual needs, moving readers forward from wherever (below, on, or above grade level) they are.

The following is a troubleshooting guide for planning instruction that is closely connected to running-record results. Effective troubleshooting is essential to supporting every child—from the underachiever to the struggling reader. Some of the suggested interventions may be used immediately—during the running-record debriefing conference—while others are more appropriate for small-group or whole-class lessons at a later time. After using the guide, you'll see how its suggestions become part of the daily nudging techniques you use when teaching and taking subsequent records. Athough most frequently used interventions have been included, the list is by no means exhaustive. Use it with colleagues as a base for adding your own collective observations and ideas.

Before You Take the Running Record

If...

...then

❊ the child appears anxious...

...go over the purpose of RRs (also a good topic for a whole-class meeting). Emphasize that what you learn about his skills will help you plan what to teach next. Explain that each child is different and is at a different reading level, and that practicing what you find out about his needs will help him improve his reading just the way practice in sports improves performance.

... remind the child of his strengths (*You're great at catching your own errors and correcting them*). Let him know that these will show up as he reads and that any mistakes he makes will help you decide together what kind of help will work best right now.

❊ the child always selects an easy text...

... remind her that you need to see how she figures out words she doesn't know. Suggest that she choose a harder book so you can do this. Go over the Goldilocks test for selecting books with her. If she keeps selecting books that are too easy, choose some yourself and tell the child that you think these will work better to show how she figures things out.

If...	...then
❋ the child always selects a particular genre for reading (i.e., narrative, picture book, informational)...	...tell the child that you've heard him read several books of that type and that you need to see how he reads with other genres or kinds of writing.
	... build in more practice time—partner reading and retelling—with other genres.

With the class or group:

...be sure to introduce different genres when you select books for teacher read-alouds.

...periodically identify a genre du jour for independent reading time.

❋ the child has difficulty making predictions about the text's content...	...spend more time bringing out or building background knowledge on the topic of the selection.
	...model how to make predictions, explaining why you made each one.
❋ the child has difficulty posing prereading questions that give him a reason to read this particular text...	...spend time exploring "What I (the child) want to learn" from this reading.
	...model how to generate questions.

With the class or group:

... increase collaborative (class) brainstorming of questions to be answered in particular readings.

During the Oral-Reading Performance:

If...	...then
❋ the child is speed reading...	... demonstrate what good pacing, phrasing, and expression sound like and why good readers pay attention to these aspects. Explain that reading too quickly makes it difficult to think along as you read.

With the class or group:

...model pacing, phrasing, and expression in your teacher read-alouds.

...provide practice with creative dramatics and readers' theater scripts. Rehearse through repeated readings, improving oral performance each time.

If...	...then
✻ the child is inventing text...	...the book may be too hard. Continue taking notes. Assess how closely the inventing matches the context and illustrations of the selection. Share your observations with the child and talk about why he's inventing. Find an easier book for another reading. Tell the child that the first book was too hard for him to read the author's words right now, but he did a fine job at telling the story (or information) in a "book-talking way."
✻ the child fails to self-correct...	...the child may not be understanding what she reads or is unaware that it's the reader's job to use fix-up strategies when meaning is lost. Failure to self-correct is a significant indicator of a reading difficulty. ...explicitly teach reading fix-up strategies. She may need you to guide her through using a strategy. If the child stops in her tracks while reading, prompt her to use specific strategies, helping her to do so as needed. **With the class or group:** ...in teacher read-alouds, frequently model how to use fix-up strategies. ...publicly congratulate readers for self-corrections and ask them to explain (to all) how and why they made them.
✻ the child frequently asks for help...	...ask the child, *What do you think the word is? What would sound right and make sense here? How can you figure it out?* ...suggest strategies he might use: *Why don't you try to ____.* Guide the child in using specific strategies, if necessary.
✻ the child cannot get back on track after making an error...	...after the child has used, or been guided to use, fix-up strategies effectively, have her reread the section with the corrections.
✻ The child is reading word by word instead of in meaningful phrases...	...ask the child to reread to make it sound like talking. ...have the child echo read (repeat what you read with the same word phrasing and expression). **With the class or group:** ...emphasize phrased reading in your teacher read-alouds. ...publicly praise effective phrase reading when children read-aloud for the class.

If...	...then
❧ the child's reading lacks expression or the expression is inappropriate...	...have the child echo read.
	...emphasize expression and intonation in your teacher read-alouds.
	...publicly praise effective expression when children read aloud for the class.
	...have the child participate in readers' theater presentations, rehearsing scripts using dramatic expression.
	...have the child read into a tape recorder, listen to and assess his own sample, then reread to improve his performance. Rereading builds sight vocabulary and fluency. Self-selected rereading activities give children a chance to practice and improve.
❧ the child repeatedly hesitates or pauses for long periods of time...	...the child may be hesitating when he approaches an unfamiliar word. Build his self confidence by having him practice and use word-attack skills independently. Support and praise his independent use of strategies.
	...build sight vocabulary, particularly high frequency words. Readers use context clues effectively when they know (and read) most of the words in the sentence instantly.
	...model think-along strategies, demonstrating how readers maintain focus and process information as they read.
❧ The child has difficulty keeping her place on the page...	...screen for visual difficulties.
	...determine whether focus is the problem and demonstrate think-along strategies.
	...allow the child to use a marker or move her finger under the line of text or down the side of the page, line by line, as she reads. Gradually, this tracking should become unnecessary.
❧ the child repeats words, phrases, lines of text, or sentences (with or without corrections) often...	...praise repetitions that are self-corrections of miscues or that clarify meaning, but emphasize that unnecessary repetitions are distracting. Explain that it's hard to understand what you read when the flow is continuously interrupted.
	...have the child listen to one of her taped readings, then reread the same passage with a focus on reducing repetitions.

If...	...then
❉ the words the child reads do not exactly match the words in the text...	...have the child finger point to each word as he reads. Gradually, he will do this tracking visually. ...have the child find and frame selected words on the page to establish and reinforce the concept of word-ness (criteria for a separate word).
❉ the reader appears unable to use, or disregards, context clues...	...model, (teacher and peers) how to process (think about) the information coming in at the phrase, sentence, and paragraph level while reading. Logical thinking—integrating background knowledge with information absorbed from the reading—leads to a natural use of context clues. The child uses these clues to decode words and word meanings. ...using examples across several texts, show typical patterns for context clues (i.e., definition by comparison—*Sam felt apprehension, just like his fearful sister*).
❉ the reader stumbles on high frequency words...	...increase shared reading, buddy reading, shared writing, and other meaningful activities that will support the reader while working with these words. ...provide ample time for the child to read easy-level books independently. ...encourage the child to reread familiar texts to practice fluency. ...include independent writing tasks providing lots of resources for word searching (word walls, personal dictionaries, and so on). **With the class or group:** ...have word activities and materials available (i.e., magnetic letters, Boggle, Scrabble). ...emphasize high frequency words when scribing for children during shared or interactive writing.
❉ the reader stumbles with technical words...	... teach technical words connected with theme units. Thoroughly discuss the words used in texts as well as their derivations and variations. ...teach structural patterns often used in technical words (i.e., ol-o-gy identifies a science).
❉ the child makes frequent substitutions...	...discuss the reader's significant substitutions, exploring why he made them and examine the author's word. ...have the child listen to his own taped reading while following the text, then reread to improve accuracy.

If...	...then
❋ the child's substitutions are meaningful, but alter shades of meaning....	...explain how the meaning was subtly changed with these substitutions and the possible misinterpretations that can occur.
❋ the substitutions do not fit grammatically in the sentence structure...	...discuss why the substitution doesn't sound right or isn't like we sequence or use words when we speak. ...reinforce the concept that, like speech, written sentences must follow an order to sound right.
❋ the substitutions are not meaningful, but reflect a use of phonetic knowledge...	...praise the child's attempt to use phonetic knowledge, but reinforce that the word must also make sense in the context. ...model how to integrate awareness of meaning from context with phonetic knowledge when decoding words.
❋ the substitutions are not meaningful and do not reflect phonetic knowledge...	...model how to integrate awareness of meaning from context with phonetic knowledge when decoding words. ...strengthen phonetic knowledge and guide the child to apply this knowledge in reading and writing activities. ...have word activities and materials available for use (i.e., magnetic letters, Boggle, Scrabble). ...have the child do more independent writing on self-selected topics. He will need to examine phonetic principles at the word level in order to get his message across.
❋ the child has left out words...	...assess the child's tracking of print—word matching. ...after the RR, draw her attention back to these words for a closer look. Explain how some omissions don't alter meaning and others do—sometimes significantly ...work on word recognition skills and vocabulary knowledge. Omissions may indicate weaknesses in these areas and an unwillingness to struggle with decoding.
❋ the child has inserted words that enhance the text...	...the text may be too unsophisticated for this child, and he is attempting to improve it. Select a more difficult text. ...the child may not be familiar with story language and is trying to modify the text to match speech patterns. Increase teacher read-alouds with discussion of book language in different genres.

...explain that when reading easy books, in order to appreciate the story line, patterns, language, illustrations, or to share with others, it's important to respect the author's words as an art form—a creation.

❋ the child has inserted words that alter meaning in some way...	...after taking the RR, draw the child's attention to these words. Repeat the child's words and ask if they make sense or fit with what the author wants to get across. Discuss how specific insertions create misunderstandings.
❋ the child has left out or misused punctuation...	...determine possible reasons for these errors. Speed reading may be a factor. (Refer to suggestions for speed reading.)
	...tell and show how authors use punctuation to guide readers through their message. Explain that the punctuation is like stage directions in a play. It tells the reader when to pause, stop, use particular emotions, and so on.

During the Retelling

If...   **...then**

❋ the child appears unaware of the expectations for retelling...	...review the retelling procedure, step by step.
	...model, (teacher and peers) retellings with different genres.
	With the class or group:
	...after introducing the scoring checklist to the class, display it for readers to use during RRs and as a guide when practicing with partners.
❋ the child lacks confidence...	...provide lots of structured practice, practice, practice with the process.
	...have the child listen to his own taped retellings and, with the checklist as a standard, determine how he can improve them.
❋ the child cannot identify the genre (Is this a story, an informational book, etc.?)...	...identify genre types in classroom texts, pointing out specific characteristics and formats for each.
❋ the child's retelling is incomplete or sketchy...	...review the procedure, step-by-step.
	...point out exactly what's missing in the child's retelling and why it's needed.

	...have the child listen to his own taped retellings and, with the checklist as a standard, determine how she can improve them.
✿ the child needs a few prompts...	...give the prompts and note what type they were, where they were needed, and how successful they were in guiding the child's retelling.
	...praise the reader's successful use of your prompts. Tell him that you hope to see self-prompting (using the posted checklist) during the next RR.
✿ the child needs to reread sections of the text, examine the illustrations, or both, during the retelling...	...explain that rereading is a good strategy for checking information, but that it's also important to recall accurately most of the information after reading. Explain that this recall shows that he's thinking and understanding what he reads as he goes along and that it improves his performance on a RR.
✿ the child's retelling does not follow the sequence of the text or a logical order (i.e., story grammar, main ideas and details)...	...explain that sometimes a specific sequence can be critical to meaning (timeline, story line) and that sometimes—when there's a collection within a section of the text (i.e., characteristics of mammals)—the order doesn't make any difference and can vary.
✿ the child's retelling shows that she doesn't understand the technical words...	...teach words associated with theme studies across content areas—including derivations and variations on meanings and forms.
	...emphasize the importance of using context clues and definitions embedded within the text.
✿ the child's retelling shows little, or no strength in making personal inferences and drawing conclusions...	...model, (teacher and peers) how to form logical inferences and draw conclusions. Use read-alouds and class discussions to demonstrate the thinking involved.
	...prompt the reader to read between and beyond the lines and guide his expression of ideas.
✿ the child makes few connections with prior knowledge and other readings...	... model, (teacher and peers) how to make logical connections. Use read-alouds and class discussions to demonstrate the thinking involved.
	...prompt the reader to explain how ideas in this reading are related to her prior knowledge and are, or are not, compatible with information from other sources.

.... *During the Debriefing Conference*

If...	...then
❧ the child appears defensive when discussing errors...	...emphasize the strengths you noted in his reading and retelling. ...once again review the purpose of the RR and error analysis. ...make a comparison to sports. After watching game films, the coach and players discuss what to practice (i.e., an outside shot at the basket).
❧ the child has difficulty expressing possible reasons for particular miscues. (i.e., explaining his thinking)...	... remind the child how in a read-aloud for the class, you discussed a miscue you'd made, and review the error (*I was expecting it to say* excited, *so I said that when I saw the* e *at the beginning and the* t *in the middle, but it was* ecstatic. Ecstatic *means very, very happy ,so it's different from* excited. *Miscues can change meaning, some more than others.*) **With the class or group:** ...after reading aloud for children, discuss a miscue you've made ...after a teacher read-aloud, have the children follow your example and collaboratively (with the class) analyze miscues they've made. This will help those children who are reluctant to examine errors, those who have difficulty finding the words to explain mistakes, and those who have limited experience in thinking about why they may have made particular errors.
❧ the child has trouble identifying goals for future performances...	... prompt the child to match areas of difficulty you and he have noted in the running record with skills you've been working on (i.e., self-correcting miscues is easier when the clunk process is used). Explain that by identifying that need, you've pinpointed an area that can be improved with more guided and independent practice. **With the class or group:** ...with a student volunteer, model a collaborative goal setting for the class. ...have children role play goal setting with a partner.

The *then* suggestions listed in this troubleshooting guide come from what works for me. The suggestions offered are a starting place for building your own expanded version. I'd love to know what you add.

Final Thoughts

Each reader I work with enlightens me about the reading process, the way literacy skills are acquired and develop, the power of collaborative evaluation and goal setting, and the effectiveness of my teaching. Integrating field experience with reading theory makes the instruction I plan relevant, timely, and more appropriate for individual learners. I've discovered that thinking together with the learner makes the analysis easier, the relationship stronger, and builds self-reflection skills that go far beyond literacy situations. Running-records have become a mainstay of my teaching. I hope that my experiences with them will help you make them an effective tool for you.

Bibliography

Baker, L. (1990). *Life in the Oceans.* NY: Scholastic.

Barr, M., Craig, D., Fisette, D., & Syverson, M. (1999). *Assessing Literacy with The Learning Record.* NH: Heinemann.

Brown, M. (1996). *Arthur Writes a Story.* MA: Little, Brown.

Brozo, W. G. (1990). "Learning how at-risk readers learn best: a case for interactive assessment." *Journal of Reading,* vol. 33, pp. 522-527.

Centre for Language in Primary Education (1989). *The Primary Language Record.* NH: Heinemann.

Clay, M. (1987). *The Early Detection of Reading Difficulties* (3rd ed.). NH: Heinemann.

Clay, M. (1993). *An Observational Survey of Early Literacy Achievement.* NH: Heinemann.

Cooper, J. D. (1993). *Literacy: Helping Children Construct Meaning.* Boston, MA: Houghton Mifflin Company.

dePaola, T. (1973). *Nana Upstairs & Nana Downstairs.* NY: Puffin Books.

Fountas, I. & Pinnell, G. (1996). *Guided Reading.* NH: Heinemann.

George, J. (1972). *Julie of the Wolves.* NY: HarperCollins Publishers.

Gillet, J. & Temple, C. (1994). *Understanding Reading Problems.* NY: HarperCollins College Press.

Goodman, Y. M. (1986). "Children Coming to Know Literacy." In W.H. Teal & E. Sulzby (Eds.), *Emergent Literacy: Reading and Writing* (pp. 1-14). Norwood, NJ: Ablex.

Goodman, Y. & Burke, C. (1972). *Reading Miscue Inventory: Procedures for Diagnosis and Evaluation.* NY: Macmillan Publishing Company.

Harris, A. & Sipay, E. (1990). *How to Increase Reading Ability.* NY: Longman.

ILEA/Centre for Language in Primary Education (London, England) (1989). *The Primary Language Record*. NH: Heinemann.

Johns, J. (1994). *Basic Reading Inventory*. Dubuque, IA: Kendall/Hunt Publishing Company.

Johnson, P. (1992). *Constructive Evaluation of Literate Activity*. NY: Longman.

Koskinen, P., Gambrell, L., Kapinus, B., & Heathington, B. (1988). "Retelling: A Strategy for Enhancing Students' Reading Comprehension." *The Reading Teacher*, vol. 41, (9).

Leslie, L. & Caldwell, J. (1990). *Qualitative Reading Inventory*. NY: HarperCollins.

Levin, E. (1993). *If You Traveled on the Underground Railroad*. NY: Scholastic.

Lipson, M. & Wixon, K. (1991). *Assessment and Instruction of Reading Disabilities*. NY: HarperCollins.

May, F. (1994). *Reading as Communication*. NY: Macmillan Publishing Company.

New York State Education Department (1999). *Early Literacy Profile*. Albany, NY: NY State Education Department.

New Zealand Ministry of Education (1996). *Reading for Life: The Learner as a Reader*. Wellington, New Zealand: Learning Media Limited.

Paul, A. (1992). *Shadows Are About*. NY: Scholastic.

Perma-Bound (1998-99). *Perma-Bound Main Catalog*. NJ: Perma-Bound Books.

Schon, D. (1983). *The Reflective Practitioner: How Professionals Think in Action*. NY: Basic Books, Inc., Publishers.

Shaw, C. (1988). *It Looked Like Spilt Milk*. NY: HarperCollins.

Tompkins, G. (1997). *Literacy for the 21st Century*. NJ: Merrill, Prentice Hall.

Thompkins, G. (1998). *Language Arts: Content and Teaching Strategies* (4th ed.). NJ: Basic Books, Inc., Publishers.

Tonkovich, M., Hanson, S., Calkins, A., & Loseby, P. (1992). *Language Arts Portfolio Handbook*. Juneau, Alaska: Juneau School District

Walker, B. (1996). *Diagnostic Teaching of Reading: Techniques for Instruction and Assessment*. NJ: Merrill, Prentice Hall.

Weaver, C. (1994). *Reading Process and Practice*, (2nd ed.). NH: Heinemann.